Reader's Digest
Wildlife Watch

Waterside & Coast in Spring

Reader's Digest
Wildlife Watch

Waterside & Coast in Spring

Published by
The Reader's Digest Association Limited
London · New York · Sydney · Montreal

Contents

Wildlife habitats and havens

Coast watch

Animals and plants in focus

Waterside watch

Introduction

Winter can be reluctant to release its grip on the land. Even as the days lengthen in March, and the first spring flowers bloom beneath the bare trees, sand martins returning to their breeding grounds from Africa often find themselves flying through late flurries of snow. These small, frail-looking relatives of swallows are among the first spring migrants from the tropics. Undeterred by the swirling snowflakes, they battle on until the glint of sunlight on water signals their arrival over their nesting sites on river banks and lake shores. Soon they are darting and swooping through the air to seize tiny flying insects. Their appearance proves beyond doubt that spring has arrived.

The insects themselves have only just hatched from the water. Aroused from winter dormancy by the warmth of the spring sun, their eggs and aquatic larvae start developing fast, and by the time the sand martins arrive the first tiny flies are swarming over the water.

◄ The dazzlingly white little egret breeds only around the estuaries of the south coast, where the mild climate encourages it to stay on through the winter. However, it is gradually spreading farther north.

▼ Also known as the water-boatman, the curious backswimmer hangs upside-down from the surface film in ponds and ditches, and uses its long, oar-like legs to dart after other insects that fall in the water.

▲ Sea campion often blooms alongside thrift and early purple orchid. It may be found close to many of the puffin colonies of western Britain.

Nesting colonies

The martins scoop up insects by the mouthful to fuel their efforts as they refurbish their old burrows or excavate new ones, digging deep into sandy cliffs above the water. These nesting colonies were once a common feature of eroded river banks, but today they are more frequently found in the flooded sand and gravel pits that dot the lowlands (see pages 16–21). Dug to provide raw material for the construction industry, these pits often mature into ideal habitats for water life.

Sand martins are soon joined by hunting swallows and house martins, and in May swifts start to arrive from Africa, heading straight for good feeding areas (see pages 50–54). While the migrants twist and turn in pursuit of aquatic insects, waterbirds such as coots and grebes perform their dramatic territorial and courtship rituals on the water below. The spectacular great crested grebe partly owes its revival in Britain to the proliferation of flooded gravel pits in recent decades.

Ringing calls

The pits that supply sand and gravel for modern industries often lie on the flood plains of rivers. In a few places, patterns of ridges and partly silted-up channels may mark the remains of water meadows. These are riverside grasslands that were artificially flooded with silt-rich water to provide a good hay crop (see pages 12–15). Where they survive, the damp meadows are often bright with wetland wild flowers, such as ragged-robin and cuckoo flower. Any remaining channels and pools are frequently almost overgrown with common reeds, bulrushes and yellow iris, yet despite this they provide ideal breeding sites for amphibians such as frogs and toads (see pages 69–73) and the more elusive smooth newt (see pages 66–68), as well as the jewel-like damselflies that start to appear on the waterside vegetation in May.

Meanwhile the reedbeds flanking the river may ring with the twanging calls of bearded tits and the chattering notes of reed warblers. In southern England a patch of willow scrub may be claimed as a breeding territory by a Cetti's warbler – a skulking, apparently secretive bird that nevertheless advertises its presence with explosive outbursts of loud, staccato

◀ Often confused with the resident grey wagtail, which also has yellow plumage, the yellow wagtail is a spring visitor to damp pastures near water, where it often feeds near the feet of grazing cattle.

▶ From May onwards the tousled, rose-pink petals of ragged-robin are often to be seen adorning overgrown water meadows that have escaped agricultural development.

▶ The elegant great crested grebe builds its nest on a floating platform of mud and tangled weeds. The nest may be supported on a fallen branch or anchored by submerged reeds.

notes. They often interrupt the softer, more insistent whirr of the grasshopper warbler, which sounds more like the spinning reel of an angler's line than a small bird. Few of these birds will show themselves, but the spring air is full of their song.

Brief lives

In the rivers, fish are rising. Watching from below, trout, dace and grayling see the water dimple as spent mayflies fall from the air and are trapped by the surface tension. Struggling feebly as they are carried downstream, these insects are soon snapped up by the hungry fish, leaving nothing but an expanding ring of ripples on the moving water. For the mayflies (see pages 74–75) this swift demise makes little difference; their lives are over anyway. They take to the air with just one aim, to mate and lay their eggs. The act of breeding exhausts all their reserves of energy, and those that are not devoured by fish will soon die.

Many of the fish that prey on the mayflies are themselves in danger. Rivers and lakes are rich hunting grounds for predators such as the mink (see pages 40–45), which was brought to Britain from America more than seventy-five years ago, and native fish-eaters, such as the otter and the pike of sinister

reputation (see pages 60–63). Danger also stalks the shallows in the form of the grey heron (see pages 46–49), another stealthy hunter that relies on a combination of patience and lightning-fast reflexes to secure its prey.

In spring, few wetlands reverberate to the strange booming calls of the bittern, a smaller, more thickset relative of the grey heron that hunts in much the same way among the reedbeds. Once numerous in the fens and marshes of lowland Britain, the bittern has suffered from the drainage of wetlands, and the breeding population, although having recently increased, is currently about 40 pairs. Today the boom of the breeding male is likely to be heard only in the remaining marshlands of East Anglia, or drifting from the reedbeds of Leighton Moss in Lancashire.

Yet while the bittern has declined, another relative of the heron has flourished. The elegant little egret is becoming an increasingly common sight on the southern fringes of Britain. Originally a rare autumn visitor from Europe, it is now a year-round resident, with 160 pairs breeding around the estuaries and salt marshes of the south coast in spring. Brackish coastal lagoons in southern and eastern England are also the breeding sites of the avocet, one of the greatest wildlife success stories of the last 60 years (see pages 86–91).

▲ Restricted to the fens of East Anglia, the rare swallowtail butterfly first emerges in May. This one is hanging from its empty chrysalis to dry its wings.

◄ Britain's largest newt, the rare and protected great crested, visits its breeding pools in spring to court a mate and spawn. The male is 15cm (6in) long and the female may reach 18cm (7in).

▲ Although it looks rather like a gull, the fulmar is a relative of the albatross family. Like these birds, it spends most of its life at sea but comes ashore to breed on cliff ledges.

Cliffs and stacks

Egrets and avocets are birds of soft, southern shores. Farther west and north, the nature of the coast changes completely. Hard rock and wild weather create ragged coastlines of cliffs, stacks and rocky reefs. Here the receding tide reveals the glittering world of the rock pool (see pages 22–27) with its intriguing variety of strange and often beautiful animals. Up on the cliffs, the windswept, salt-drenched rocks provide rootholds for a mosaic of lichens (see pages 116–120), some of the toughest and most tenacious of all organisms. Farther up, pockets of soil in rock crevices support cushions of thrift, with their rounded heads of pink flowers, while the yellow-green blooms of alexanders can be seen on the more sheltered, gentler slopes. On some cliff tops the vegetation forms a distinctive habitat known as coastal heath (see pages 28–31), in which heather and gorse grow alongside maritime plants such as thrift and sea campion.

In late spring the more remote cliffs and islands provide one of the year's greatest wildlife spectacles when they are colonised by thousands of breeding seabirds. Kittiwakes, guillemots, razorbills, fulmars and shags seem to occupy every narrow ledge and crevice, building gravity-defying nesting sites that combine easy access to the sea with virtually impregnable security from predators such as foxes and stoats. All these birds are creatures of the ocean. They come ashore to breed, and cling to the fringes of the land for only as long as it takes to rear their young. Only a few venture much farther inland than the cliff face – they include the puffin (see pages 92–97) that nests in burrows on the cliff tops, often in company with rabbits, the gannets that take over the tops of small islands, and the terns that form large breeding colonies on shingle shores and grassy strands.

These spring seabird colonies are among the most important in the world – some 70 per cent of the world's gannet population nests on British and Irish coasts and islands. Tragically, there have been several major breeding failures in recent years, attributed to a lack of prey – principally sand eels – caused by a combination of overfishing and rising sea temperatures. Yet the breeding colonies are still breathtaking demonstrations of the vigour and wild beauty of the natural world, and are among the most compelling reasons for visiting the coast in spring.

▲ In general, damselflies emerge earlier than their larger relatives, the dragonflies. The large red damselfly is one of the first to take to the air, and is often to be seen perched near the water.

▲ In spring many marine animals move into shallow water, and species such as the broad-clawed porcelain crab can be found in rock pools and beneath stones on the lower shore.

▶ Some rocky western coasts of the British Isles are home to the chough. It belongs to the crow family and feeds mainly on insects gathered from short, rabbit-cropped, cliff-top turf.

Wildlife habitats and havens

- Water meadows
- Gravel pits
- Life in a rock pool
- Coastal heath
- The Wye Valley

Water meadows

Hosts of colourful spring flowers transform flooded pastures into fertile breeding grounds for bees, butterflies and grasshoppers. Occasionally, the distinctive chirp of a bush cricket may be heard above the hum of insect life.

Many lowland rivers are prone to flooding. As the water spreads out over the surrounding land, it deposits nutrient-rich silt, carried by the current from farther upstream. The silt enriches the soil, promoting the growth of grasses and other plants. In winter, the flood waters protect the grass from the worst of the cold weather and stimulate early growth in spring.

The benefits of this natural but rather haphazard winter flooding gave farmers the idea of controlling the flood waters in order to create artificial water meadows. A carefully planned system of dams and sluices was employed to divert water from the main river channel on to nearby grassland, and then return it to the river lower down.

A series of shallow ridges running across the meadow at right angles to the main stream ensured that the water flowed slowly over the meadow, giving it time to deposit its silt before returning to the main channel.

The sluices enabled the flooding to be timed to protect the new growth from frost, and ensured that the meadow could be drained when the spring sun was strong enough for the grass to grow well. Kept free of grazing livestock in spring, the land was used to grow a hay crop that was cut in early summer, after most of the plants had flowered and set seed. The

▼ Many grasses, rushes and flowers flourish in the damp, uncultivated soil of a water meadow that flanks a lowland river.

▲ The flowers of water forget-me-not gleam pale blue among the tall grasses of water meadows. Each tiny bloom has a golden eye at its centre.

▶ Cuckoo flower is a common plant of damp grassland. It is avoided by grazing animals because of its bitter-tasting leaves, but it is a vital foodplant for the orange-tip butterfly.

▲ Adult scarlet tiger moths appear in June. Before then, their caterpillars feed on water meadow plants such as comfrey and meadowsweet.

▶ On breezy days, the air is full of dandelion seeds being blown away from the spherical seed-heads, each one supported by its own fluffy white parachute.

▲ Water meadow flowers provide a vital source of nectar and pollen for foraging bees, as well as butterflies and other insects.

meadow was then used for grazing until it was time to flood it again.

These artificially created water meadows were a product of an era when farm labour was cheap and tasks such as haymaking were carried out using scythes and rakes and other hand tools. Water meadows are quite unsuited to modern mechanised farming, and they have mostly fallen into disuse. Many have been drained and fertilised and are used for growing crops. Some still survive, however. Even though the artificial flooding regime has been abandoned, they are still prone to natural winter flooding, and have often been left untended.

Even though it has become increasingly rare, the water vole still feeds by the ditches and streams that pass through water meadows. It slips into the water at the first hint of disturbance.

Similar tracts of naturally wet grasslands can also be found – so-called 'unimproved' flood meadow and grazing marsh that have escaped drainage and cultivation. Rich in grassland wildlife, they are wonderful places to explore in spring, when the air is full of birdsong and the flowers are at their most colourful.

Meadow flowers

Marsh marigold and lesser spearwort often provide the most striking displays in spring and early summer. Their brilliant yellow petals attract insects, especially bees, but their foliage is poisonous to grazing animals and therefore avoided, enabling them to flourish at the expense of other, more palatable plants. Dandelions are also common

in water meadows, usually in slightly raised areas where the soil is not so wet. They are sometimes the dominant flowers for several weeks. Greater bird's-foot trefoil scrambles over grasses and sedges, contributing to the predominantly yellow effect. Another frequently occurring species is common meadow rue, a tall plant with strong-smelling, dense green foliage and frothy yellow flowerheads. Its tiny flowers have white petals with conspicuous yellow stamens.

Ragged robin often adds a splash of pink to the meadow. This relative of red campion has deeply divided petals, each cut into four lobes, giving it the somewhat tattered appearance that accounts for its name. It is an important foodplant for the caterpillars of the common forester moth, a vibrant green day-flying moth that thrives in unimproved meadows.

Another common spring flower that brings early interest to the meadow is the cuckoo flower, or lady's smock. White at a distance, it reveals a delicate veining of pink and purple when examined closely.

White haze

Grouped in clusters on delicate scrambling stems, the minute flowers of marsh bedstraw give the appearance of a white haze floating over the grasses. The fragrant honey-like scent of these

▲ Grey herons are attracted to water meadows because there are usually plenty of fish and frogs to be caught in the water and in the damp grass.

SNAKE'S-HEAD FRITILLARY

One of the most distinctive plants to be found growing on water meadows is the snake's-head fritillary. This little flower, with its dusky hanging bells chequered with mulberry and lilac, once grew by the thousand in ancient pastures. Yet it was always considered special and was given a variety of country names including sulky ladies, chequered lily and, more morbidly, leper's bells.

Today, the snake's-head fritillary grows wild only on a few protected sites in the south, such as Magdalen College Meadow in Oxford. Where it does occur, however, it often grows in great numbers, creating a cloud of purple over the meadow grasses.

Careful management is essential to the survival of all wild flowers, including the snake's-head fritillary. They can produce seed only if the meadow is left uncut or ungrazed until well into the summer. Cutting meadows early to make silage prevents the plants setting seed, and overgrazing can also reduce the number and variety of wild flowers.

Hidden within the angular pinkish purple flowers, the bright yellow stamens of snake's-head fritillary are usually visible only to visiting insects.

Large colonies of snake's-head fritillary often contain white flowers as well as the usual chequered blooms of deep purple.

▲ White spikes of marsh helleborine may appear in damper meadows in late summer. In the right conditions it can form extensive colonies.

flowers fills the evening air, attracting small pollinating insects. By contrast, water forget-me-not produces an abundance of sky-blue flowers, each with a yellow 'eye' in the centre. These colourful blooms can be seen throughout the summer both in the meadow and on the banks of the stream itself. They are complemented by the deep blue, rounded heads

◄ A plentiful supply of insects, worms and small fish attracts the little water shrew, which is around 7–9.5cm (3–4in) long.

of devil's-bit scabious and the deep reddish brown flower spikes of greater burnet. However, they are all dwarfed by the lofty marsh thistle – at up to 3m (10ft), this is the tallest of all meadow flowers.

Orchids thrive in water meadows, benefiting from the rich, damp soil. The early marsh orchid, with its pinkish flowers, is one of the first species in bloom, followed closely by the southern marsh orchid. This handsome plant has deep magenta flowers, and may be so abundant that it turns whole

meadows purple. Several other orchids also occur in damp meadows, including the diminutive green-winged orchid and the common spotted orchid.

Insect paradise
The many nectar-rich flowers attract a host of hoverflies, bees, butterflies and moths, making water meadows among the best places to look for flying insects in spring and early summer. Moths such as the scarlet tiger may be disturbed in long grass, while others such as the drinker and scarce forester can be found later in the summer. China-mark moths, the caterpillars of which feed on aquatic plants, are also common on the waterside vegetation.

Grasshoppers and bush crickets crowd the long grass, their calls adding to the hum of insect life. They include the long-winged cone-head, a bush cricket that has recently increased its range in Britain and is becoming more widespread in damp meadows. Leaf-green in colour, and consequently very difficult to spot among long grass, its high-pitched chirping is usually the only clue to its whereabouts. If it is disturbed

▲ Shy and elusive, the water rail conceals its nest among the reeds in marshy areas of the meadow. It has a distinctive squealing call, but is rarely seen.

► The southern marsh orchid is one of the most typical plants of water meadows and similar wetland habitats in southern England.

▲ A careful search of damp vegetation, especially close to open water, may reveal the amber snail – a mere 17mm (¾in) high – among the leaves.

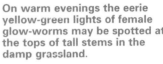

On warm evenings the eerie yellow-green lights of female glow-worms may be spotted at the tops of tall stems in the damp grassland.

Despite a significant decline in its numbers, the common snipe can still be found nesting in the long grass in undisturbed areas of water meadows.

it stops calling and drops down into the vegetation, emerging only when it senses that the danger has passed.

One of the most intriguing insects to be found in damp meadows is the glow-worm. This species – which is actually a beetle and not a worm at all – was common in the British Isles about 50 years ago, but its numbers have been reduced dramatically by habitat loss. It is still widespread, however, especially in southern England, where it often occurs in water meadows. The glow-worm takes its name from the greenish light emitted from the tip of the abdomen by the wingless female. During the day the females hide in dense grass, but as night falls they climb up grass stems to display their light and attract a winged male with which to mate.

Feeding birds

In winter, partly flooded water meadows provide ideal conditions for wildfowl and waders. Dabbling ducks such as teal and wigeon are common, while waders such as snipe and redshank are likely to be seen near the water. Grey herons stalk the shallows in search of fish, and flocks of lapwings work their way over the damp ground looking for insects and worms.

The yellow wagtail is a declining summer visitor, nesting on the ground in the long grass. Meadow pipits and skylarks are also ground-nesting species that may breed in some of the drier meadows. Water pipits feed – but don't breed – around the margins

and moorhens and coots are often to be seen searching for food along the feeder streams. Even rare migrant waders, such as the lesser yellowlegs from North America, turn up from time to time, especially near the coast or large rivers.

Losing ground

Huge areas of water meadow and damp pasture have been drained and ploughed up in recent decades, making the surviving meadows especially precious. Many are protected sites, carefully managed to maintain water levels and conserve their rich flora. On spring days, when the sun is glinting off the water, they are among the most enchanting of all wildlife havens.

Seasonally flooded grassland is grazed by cattle in summer, after spring flowers have set seed and most chicks of ground-nesting birds have fledged.

WILDLIFE WATCH

Where can I see water meadows?

● Most of the surviving water meadows are to be found in the south of England. One of the best sites to visit is North Meadow National Nature Reserve at Cricklade in Wiltshire. Flanking the upper reaches of the Thames, it supports a vast colony of snake's-head fritillaries.

● Amberley Wild Brooks near Arundel in West Sussex is a large area of wet grassland and water meadow that regularly floods in winter, and attracts thousands of wildfowl and waders.

● Winnall Moors, a former water meadow beside the River Itchen near Winchester, has varied wildlife. It is managed by Hampshire Wildlife Trust, and guided walks led by the warden can be arranged. Telephone 01489 774400 or visit www.hwt.org.uk

Gravel pits

Overgrown with grasses and reeds, an abandoned gravel pit becomes a sanctuary for ducks, geese and waders, while a quarry's newly dug cliffs and banks provide sand martins with an ideal place for excavating breeding burrows.

Sand and gravel pits are a dominant feature of the countryside in several parts of lowland Britain, where thick deposits of sand and river gravel lie close to towns and cities. The pits are needed to supply the construction industry. Huge amounts of concrete are constantly required for roads, airports and buildings. Concrete is composed of cement and ballast, which is a mixture of sand and gravel. This means that immense quantities of sand and gravel need to be excavated each year. While they are being actively worked, these pits are busy industrial sites. Once they are exhausted or abandoned, however, many fill with water and become overgrown with vegetation, which transforms them into peaceful places for a variety of insects, birds, fish, reptiles, amphibians and occasionally mammals to take up residence. Even dry pits provide havens for specialist plants and animals.

Nesting opportunities

Historically, gravel pits were quite small and often served local needs only. In areas where gravel deposits were common, many communities had a 'parish pit' where local people could go to take what they needed, paying a small sum to parish funds. Today, gravel extraction is a multi-million pound industry involving sophisticated machinery. The material is often removed by draglines, working on the bottom of dry pits or from the banks of wet pits. In other cases, it is dug by dredgers mounted on the banks or on floating pontoons.

The machines involved in these processes have interesting nooks and crannies, and are often chosen as nesting places by birds such as the pied wagtail. Occasionally, these birds may even nest successfully in machinery that moves from place to place, provided it moves slowly enough. Bigger holes can be used by bigger birds, of course, and the shelter provided by disused machinery is sometimes exploited by such larger birds as jackdaws and barn owls.

Flooded gravel pits may look like a haphazard collection of shallow lakes and islands but they often have a complicated structure. The varying depths, gradients and channels cater for the requirements of many different wildlife species.

Sand martin colonies

An important part of the extraction process is the stage when the very finest silts are washed out of the valuable sands and gravels. The heaps of washed sand are sometimes colonised by sand martins, which have been known to dig their holes overnight in the heaps.

The sand martin is the smallest member of the swallow family that occurs in Britain. It is brown above and white below, apart from a distinctive brown breast-band, and is therefore quite easy to tell apart from other martins and swallows.

The sand martins return from their wintering sites just south of the Sahara, in Senegal and other West African countries, in late March and April. Sand and gravel pits provide them with vital breeding sites. Natural sand cliffs, which used to occur where winter spates eroded stream and river banks, have become increasingly rare. Today many such channels have been lined with concrete. In working quarries, newly excavated sand cliffs and banks – as well as the washed heaps – make excellent substitutes. The birds need a bank at least 2m (6ft) high, with a vertical face to protect them from ground predators. They may use holes they have dug in previous years, where these are still available, but mostly they dig new nest holes each year because the old ones can get infested with parasites.

ROOSTING IN REEDBEDS

The muddy waste material that has been excavated from the gravel pit is often returned to it and makes an excellent foundation for the growth of common reeds. Once established, these plants form thick, vertical thickets that are used by a variety of birds for both breeding and roosting.

Birds need secure and warm places in which to roost at night. Many species disperse into bushes, trees, nooks and crannies, either singly or as family parties. Others choose to spend the night together in large flocks, especially outside the breeding season. Such communal roosts offer safety in numbers. During the day, large flocks provide individual birds with the opportunity to discover more feeding areas.

Many species favour reedbeds, and the reeds that often surround disused gravel workings are ideal. Reeds grow in water, so the birds are safe from ground predators. In winter the air is warmer close to the water. Swallows, sand martins and yellow wagtails frequently roost in reedbeds before and during their migrations. In winter the beds are used by resident birds such as pied wagtails and reed buntings. Starlings regularly descend on reedbeds to roost in huge noisy flocks. Their aerial displays advertise the roosting site to other birds in the locality.

▶ A plentiful supply of insects close to the water makes gravel pits very attractive to yellow wagtails. These birds can catch insects on the wing or snap them up from the ground.

▶ Common reed (*Phragmites australis*) is the largest grass in Britain. As well as providing roosting sites it plays an important role in stabilising the banks of flooded gravel pits.

▲ Starlings are highly social birds. They form large flocks, particularly in winter, and often associate with other species, such as lapwings, that also favour the disturbed ground of gravel pits.

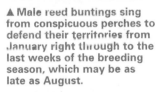

▲ Male reed buntings sing from conspicuous perches to defend their territories from January right through to the last weeks of the breeding season, which may be as late as August.

The adaptable pied wagtail is quick to take advantage of the food and shelter provided by gravel pits.

The lakes and pools that form in gravel pits are frequently the only places in a particular neighbourhood that are suitable for specialist water birds, such as the coot and the moorhen. These two species are members of the rail family, related to the shy water rail and rare corncrake. Moorhens and coots are easily told

▼ Coots build their nests in shallow water, and readily take to artificial nesting platforms.

apart. The moorhen will rarely stray far from the cover of reeds or other vegetation round the edges of the pit. It has red and yellow on its bill and white undertail coverts, which it flicks constantly up and down.

The coot is bigger and has a conspicuous white shield on its forehead, extending up from its white bill. Coots generally prefer to be out in the middle of the water, where they dive down for food.

▲ Moorhens often rear two or three broods in a season. The young of the first brood may stay to help feed and look after their younger siblings, gaining valuable experience that helps them when they come to raise their own families.

The two commonest diving ducks on gravel pits are the tufted duck and the bigger pochard. Of the two, the tufted duck is a much more common breeding bird. Male tufted ducks are strikingly black and white, while females are

▼ Tufted ducks can feed in quite deep water, diving to collect animals that live in the mud on the bottom of the lake.

duller, being two shades of brown. Both sexes of pochard have a basically grey body, but the male has a bright chestnut head and neck and black breast, while the female is brown and grey.

Perhaps the most spectacular waterbird to be seen on gravel pits is the stunning great crested grebe. The species has increased greatly in numbers over the last century, partly due to the number of gravel pit lakes that

▲ Pochard have greatly benefited from the creation of gravel pits, and in some areas the pit lakes are the only places where they live.

have been created. In spring its elaborate, dancing courtship displays are wonderful to watch. Finally, there is always the chance of seeing the electric blue flash of a kingfisher, which finds the small fish in the pits an irresistible attraction.

Great crested grebes feed on small fish, and usually swim far enough away from each other so that they do not compete for the same prey.

Sand martins dig nesting holes in a quarry's exposed banks, feeding on midges that swarm over the area. Each tunnel may be up to 1m (3ft) long, with a nesting chamber at the end lined with grass and feathers.

If a high build-up of scree accumulates beneath the cliff, this may make a breeding colony vulnerable to predators. In some cases conservationists have seen this happening, and have been able to spend an hour or two clearing the scree. Owners of working pits are often willing to provide machinery for this purpose, because if the martins move elsewhere in the vicinity, they can interfere with the commercial operation of the pit. Sand martins digging their breeding tunnels in already washed sand heaps,

The jack snipe feeds by probing in mud for worms, insects and snails. Smaller than the common snipe, it can be very difficult to see as it crouches among the waterside plants. It does not breed in Britain.

for instance, are a cause of great frustration to the pit operators, because since the nesting birds are immediately protected by law, the newly cleaned sand cannot be used. As a result, in many cases special breeding cliffs are prepared for the birds in the spring, in secluded parts of the site where they can breed without interference.

The pits that attract most sand martins are those that have been flooded, and this is because the water attracts plenty of insects. In common with swifts, swallows and house martins, sand martins feed on flying insects wherever they can find them, and since so many insects breed on or near water, flooded pits make ideal hunting grounds.

Flooded pits

Almost every gravel pit contains some water. It may take the form of a few shallow ponds or a broad lake, but either way the edges are very important for wildlife. Colonising weeds are soon followed by scrub willow and other shrubs, providing an excellent nursery for a variety of insects. These in turn attract a wide range of birds, both to breed and to feed while on migration.

Working in a small willow bed, bird ringers have been known to capture up to 200 birds in one morning. Reed warblers and sedge warblers are usually in the majority, but large numbers of willow warblers and chiffchaffs, whitethroats, lesser whitethroats, garden warblers and a few grasshopper warblers may also be there. In late summer gravel pits attract moulting adult whinchats.

The water's edge also attracts many waders, which pass through on migration. Well-vegetated margins are particularly favoured by snipe and, in winter, jack snipe. Some common seashore waders are

often found farther inland among more open margins. The records of dunlin seen inland on gravel pits and similar sites probably reflect a widespread migration from coast to coast across the country. These birds are most commonly seen in April and, during the autumn, in September and October.

Another wader that regularly visits gravel-pit edges is the green sandpiper. It passes through Britain from March to May on its way from winter quarters in Africa to its breeding grounds farther north in Europe, and again from June to October on the return journey. A few non-breeding birds stay for spring and summer.

Swifts, swallows and martins swoop low over gravel-pit lakes to feed on the insects that have hatched from the water, while ducks, grebes, coots and moorhens feed on and below the surface. The depth of the water is very important to these birds. Coots, diving ducks and grebes need quite deep water, whereas dabbling ducks, such as teal, mallard and moorhens, need shallower water where they can feed from the surface.

Kingfishers like to perch directly above the water, so they can plunge down to catch any small fish they see swimming below.

Ideally, pits should have deep areas with shallow, gently sloping edges, and a few islands so that birds such as terns and waders can find predator-free breeding sites. If any trees are growing nearby to provide a perch or two, kingfishers may find gravel pits ideal hunting grounds.

Flooded pits also provide valuable breeding sites for dragonflies, such as the southern hawker. The blue and black males of this big, powerful species are highly territorial, patrolling back and forth and investigating any intruders, including human ones. In the water itself, the big swan mussel may establish itself in large numbers. The largest examples of this bivalve mollusc may be 23cm (9in) long and more than 20 years old, so they are found only in the older pits, which also tend to have more mud on the bottom.

The churned ground on the bottom of a gravel pit can support many rare plants that are generally no longer able to survive on arable farmland. One such plant is the common spotted orchid, which often becomes established quite quickly and can form spectacular beds of pink spiky flowers in late May and June.

Planning ahead

The eventual shape and depth of a new pit is often partly determined by pre-existing footpaths, roads, railways, pylon foundations and other 'no-go zones', but nowadays excavation plans often make provision for wildlife. This can involve some compromises on the part of the pit operators, because leaving shallow areas and islands may mean that they have to sacrifice 10 to 15 per cent of the available gravel. However, planning permission for commercial

◄ The flowers of the common spotted orchid come in many shades, from white and pale pink to deep pink or purple.

► Purple loosestrife provides a splash of rich colour on the margins of flooded gravel pits.

IN THE DEPTHS

For many people, especially anglers, the most important inhabitants of gravel pits are fish.

The fish living in some pits have arrived naturally from adjacent rivers or streams, either directly or during floods. Some even arrive as eggs, transported on the feet or plumage of water birds.

However, in most cases the water will have been stocked by anglers, often with carp, tench and bream. The carp may be of one or several varieties – mirror and crucian carp are favourites –

and may have come from local sources or from far away. Indeed, commercial fisheries sometimes import specimen carp from the Continent, at great expense. The tench and bream will have come from local sources, and they will be preyed upon by local pike.

Young fish need a variety of small animals on which to feed, so they benefit from a varied habitat and an assortment of water plants to attract snails and insects. The productivity of these gravel pit fisheries can be

very high, but the size of the fish in the water depends on the fishing pressure from anglers, birds and predatory fish. When non-human predators remove a large proportion of the young fish, those that escape can get enough food to grow larger. So although anglers often blame pike or fish-eating birds for their lack of success, the presence of these predators usually ensures that the water contains much larger fish, even if there are fewer of them.

▲ Bream are bottom feeders, eating mainly insect larvae but also molluscs, freshwater shrimps and slaters.

◄ The pike preys on other fish by lurking in ambush among the water plants. When unwary prey swims close enough, the pike darts out of hiding to snatch it in its wide mouth.

▼ Tench feed on crustaceans, worms, molluscs and insect larvae, especially midge larvae, which they take mainly at night.

Water lilies grow in nutrient-rich water that is up to about 3m (10ft) deep. Their large, showy flowers attract a variety of insects, particularly beetles.

excavation may demand that the excavators make careful plans for restoring or rehabilitating the site after they have finished working it.

Often, older pits were not dug deeper than around 3m (10ft) because the aim was to refill them and turn them back into farmland. As a result many potentially valuable wildlife sites were lost, and ironically the resulting farmland was rarely very productive. Unfortunately, the demand for landfill sites is such that the value of the sand and gravel can be eclipsed by the value of the hole they came from, so many worked-

▼ After the gravel is dug from a river valley, the pits fill with ground water to form lakes, adding a new dimension to the landscape.

out sand and gravel pits are still used as dumping grounds for refuse and other material.

However, current planning practice often favours using such sites as amenities – either sports facilities, nature reserves or both. Many sites consist of several pits, allowing some to be devoted to wildlife while others are used for fishing,

► Dragonflies lay their eggs in water. The wingless nymphs that hatch from the eggs live on the bottom and among water weeds. Like the adults, they are voracious predators. After one or two years they climb out of the water before their last moult, and then emerge as brightly coloured winged adults.

sailing and water skiing. Some of these sports activities are compatible with wildlife conservation and can be integrated at one site, but others are very disruptive – ducks and water skiing, for example, do not mix.

Exploitation for minerals is often seen as more destructive of the natural environment than, say, farming. Yet the variety of wildlife found on agricultural land may be very poor, and large areas of single crops that are regularly sprayed with pesticides have little value for native wildlife. By contrast, properly managed gravel pits can contain plenty of natural habitats, providing refuges for animals and plants that are becoming scarce in an overcrowded landscape.

WILDLIFE WATCH

Where can I see gravel pits?

● Gravel pits come in all shapes and sizes. They occur in river valleys where there are thick beds of river sand and gravel, and also in areas where there are suitable glacial deposits.

● Look at detailed Ordnance Survey maps to locate pits in an area. Use the latest maps, because the shape and size of pits may change. Search areas where the map shows pits to have been in the past, as well as pits that are currently being worked.

● On the ground, the tall, gravity-fed cleaning plant is often the best indication of a working pit. Access may have been negotiated by a local birdwatching club, or there may be a footpath crossing it giving good views. Alternatively, the pit may have been worked out and have become a local amenity. Avoid pits without public access routes, because they can be highly dangerous places.

● Remember that birds and other animals may be used to the movements of men working with machines, but completely unused to other, very different actions. Try to use the cover provided by the fringing reeds and willows, and remember that for a better view, the light should come from behind you rather than in front.

● If several people regularly watch at a pit, it may be possible – with permission – to club together and build a simple hide in the best place for watching the birds. For more information, telephone the RSPB on 01767 680551 or visit www.rspb.org Keep a log book in the hide in order to keep track of the numbers of resident and migrant birds.

Life in a rock pool

Along rocky shores, pools full of marine life are replenished regularly by the tide, bringing fish, jellyfish and the occasional octopus to share the salty water with anemones, barnacles and crabs.

As the tide recedes from a rocky shore twice a day, it leaves pools of seawater among the ridges of wave-eroded rock. These rock pools can often look almost empty at first glance, apart from fronds of seaweed draped over their rocky walls, but after a few seconds tiny movements become apparent, and before long it is clear that the water is alive with small animals. Some are so well camouflaged that they are unrecognisable, and others have transparent bodies so they are all but invisible. Many look more like plants than animals, or even resemble part of the rock itself. Their abundance and variety show that many rock pools are fertile habitats, yet the reasons for this are not at all evident.

Hazardous places

Even on a bright spring morning, when the light is glinting off the water and the pools resemble exquisite natural aquaria, it is obvious that rock pools are temporary havens. In just a few hours' time, the rock and its pools will be submerged beneath the tide, and subject to the pandemonium of waves crashing over the reef, swirling through the gullies and battering their sides with loose sand and pebbles.

Any animal caught in such a maelstrom must be tough to survive, while at low tide the pool may be exposed to environmental changes that are beyond the experience of most marine organisms. When, for instance, the heat of the midday sun coincides with low water, pure water evaporates from the pool and makes the remaining water far more salty than the sea. Conversely, rain can dilute the water so it becomes almost fresh, and in the depths of winter the pool may freeze.

Yet at every high tide the surge and sluice of the waves saturates the water with life-giving oxygen and provides the pools with a virtually limitless supply of food. As long as the animals can cope with anything the

Many pools on the seashore support several different types of seaweed. These are firmly attached to the rocks by a strong 'holdfast'.

▲ One of the more surprising rock pool residents is the tompot blenny. Its large bulging eyes give it a good all-round view of danger, and a pair of curious bristly tentacles help its disguise as a weed-encrusted rock.

▶ The aptly named jewel anemone often lives in large clusters, creating dazzling splashes of underwater colour in rock pools on the lower shore. Such pools are exposed only by the very low tides that occur twice a month.

sea and exposure to the air can generate, a rock pool provides them with everything they need. So the creatures have the chance to flourish and multiply in this dangerous environment, and since only the fittest survive, they have evolved a whole suite of adaptations to help them.

Pyramid-shaped shells

Many rock-pool animals have developed tough shells that solve the two main hazards of life on rocky shores – the battering of the waves and the risk of drying out at low tide. They include the limpets, snail-like molluscs with an extremely strong pyramid-shaped shell that has evolved to deflect the force of breaking waves. They are legendary for their ability to cling to rock faces, attaching themselves with a sucker so efficient that it is virtually immune to the force of the waves. This adaptation serves to protect them from predators, such as sea birds, which cannot prise them off once they have clamped themselves tightly to the rock. It also helps the

limpets to retain water if left high and dry by the retreating tide. Limpets often live on such exposed rocks, but they also occur in rock pools where they have the opportunity to feed at any state of the tide.

A limpet is generally inactive during the hours of daylight, but at night it becomes bolder. Head and tentacles emerge from beneath the limpet's shell and the animal creeps across the rock like a snail, looking for food. It seeks tiny algae or other encrusting organisms that it can scrape off with its rasping tongue, or radula, leaving regular scratches in neat arcs. At the approach of dawn, when seabirds start to search for food, the limpet makes its way back to its starting point and clamps itself down again on the rock.

Sticking tight

The barnacles that live in large colonies around rock pools look superficially like limpets, since they too have conical shells that resist the force of the waves. A closer look reveals that their structure is quite

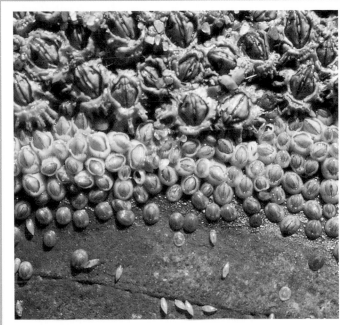

The 19th-century Swiss zoologist Louis Agassiz described a barnacle as 'nothing more than a little shrimp-like animal, standing on its head in a limestone house and kicking food into its mouth'. Yet barnacles are extraordinarily successful, covering such vast areas of coastal rock that they change the colour of the shoreline. When old

Barnacle colonies grow outwards from the edges as young barnacles settle on the rock and begin to secrete their tough conical shells.

barnacles die and fall away young ones soon settle to take their place, feeding on the plankton in the water and forming dense colonies on rocks that are too exposed for other animals.

▲ Intolerant of prolonged exposure, the apparently neon-striped blue-rayed limpet is to be found exposed only at the lowest tides.

▶ A cornered shore crab will not hesitate to use its pincers if it is molested or picked up. Common on all shores throughout Britain, it often scavenges for scraps over the exposed rocks, carrying a supply of oxygenated water in its gill chamber.

In gullies and crevices on the low-tide line, waving masses of bright green seaweeds can often be seen.

▲ Like all crustaceans, the common shrimp has ten leg-like appendages that are modified in various ways, and two pairs of antennae – the second of which are very long. It ranges in colour from dark grey to dirty yellow.

◄ Dog whelks feed on mussels and barnacles by boring through their shells and devouring the flesh within. Whelk shells vary considerably in colour, and in the size of the aperture. This is larger in dog whelks that live on very exposed shores, allowing the muscular foot to get a better grip on the rocks and stop the animals being washed away by the waves.

► The shell of the sting winkle is strong enough to withstand being trodden on, and is well able to survive rough seas.

A species of the lower shore, the painted top shell is occasionally exposed by the very lowest tides. Its shell is often washed up on the shore after the animal has died.

different, however. Each barnacle resembles a tiny volcano with sliding doors closing a vent at the top. The doors conceal a creature that is quite unlike a limpet – a crustacean that is a relative of shrimps and crabs. Like them it has jointed legs and starts life as a free-swimming animal. As it approaches maturity it settles on a rock, gluing itself in place, and develops its protective armour of plates and sliding doors. It stays cemented to that spot for the rest of its life. When it is covered by water, either at high tide or in the confines of a rock pool, it opens the sliding doors and extends its legs to gather food.

Shore zones

Thanks to their waterproof shells, common limpets and barnacles are able to survive long periods of exposure, so they are a feature of rocks and pools towards the upper part of the shore. Lower down the shore, nearer the low-tide line, the less demanding conditions enable a different set of organisms to thrive, although some of these may be closely related to the tougher animals of the upper shore.

For example, top shells – so-named because they are shaped like spinning-tops – are common inhabitants of rock pools. The flat top shell, which has wide zebra-stripes on its shell, will tolerate more exposure than the grey top shell, identifiable by its finer stripes, so one lives in pools on the upper shore and the other lives on the lower shore.

A third species, the toothed top shell – very dark and twice the size of the others – can be found even higher on the shore, where it may be covered by the sea for only a very short time on each tide. In total contrast, the colourful, conical painted top shell occurs only in pools towards the very bottom of the shore.

Killer snails

Top shells and limpets eat algae, but two other marine snails, not closely related to either of these, are carnivorous. The dog whelk and sting winkle are often found in rock pools, where they can sometimes be seen attacking other molluscs such as mussels. Their technique is to straddle their helpless prey and apply a corrosive solution to its shell. They then rasp away at the weakened shell with their toothed radulas to expose the flesh inside. They attack barnacles as well as molluscs, forcing the door-plates open after weakening them with shell-destroying fluid.

Stinging tentacles

Almost every rock pool provides a home for sea anemones, which are relatives of corals and jellyfishes. The dominant species in upper-shore pools is the beadlet anemone, which is usually deep red, although some are green and others are brown or orange-brown. A closely related but larger species is the strawberry anemone, which has small greenish spots all over its red body.

These anemones are able to survive out of water by withdrawing their tentacles into their bodies, but in rock pools they can often be seen with their tentacles extended for feeding. The tentacles are charged with thousands of microscopic stinging cells equipped with tiny barbs. When triggered by the touch of a small animal the cells pierce the animal's skin and inject a poison to paralyse it. The tentacles then transfer the prey to the anemone's mouth.

Some more stable rock pools contain snakelocks anemones, sometimes in

HOMING LIMPETS

Each limpet has a particular spot on the rock where it habitually settles. Its shell-edge is tailored to fit the irregularities of that one place. When it leaves this spot to find food its foot secretes a mucous trail as a lubricant over the rough surface – just like that of a land snail – and it follows the trail home at the end of each foraging trip.

If the trail is removed, the limpet loses its way. It wanders randomly until it comes upon its trail again, or has the good fortune to find itself back at its own spot. If it fails to find its way home, it just has to settle where it can, but since its shell does not fit the rock it runs a much greater risk of being dislodged and eaten.

Limpets clamp to the rock in so-called 'homing scars', from which they are all but impossible to detach. Not only is the suction very powerful, but the depression in the rock means that would-be predators cannot get a grip on the edge of the shell to prise it away from the surface.

Sea anemones

The symmetry of their waving tentacles can make sea anemones resemble flowers, but they are in fact simple animals that use their stinging fronds to prey on other marine creatures.

If a beadlet anemone is exposed to the air at low tide it withdraws its delicate, vulnerable tentacles into its jelly-like body and seals itself up to prevent water loss. It can stay like this for several hours until the rising water allows it to emerge.

Once submerged by the tide, the anemone puts out a fringe of tentacles to ensnare prey and drag it into its mouth. Almost any passing small animals are potential meals, including shrimps and small crabs, fish and molluscs, as well as tiny animals drifting in the water.

Stinging cells in the tentacles paralyse the prey, and the anemone then swallows and digests it. A few animals have acquired a tolerance to the stings, and one species of sea spider actually lives attached to the stems of dahlia anemones, feeding on their soft tissues.

▲ Unlike most of its relatives, the snakelocks anemone rarely retracts its tentacles fully. This makes it vulnerable to drying out, so it can survive only in rock pools that are never completely empty of water.

▶ Most common on western shores in Britain, the strawberry anemone favours shallow rocky coasts and is often to be found in rock pools.

▲ The painted goby is well camouflaged among the gravel and stones, where it attaches itself by means of pelvic fins modified into a sucker.

► Sponges such as the breadcrumb sponge are the very simplest form of multicellular animal life. Their bodies are composed of loose associations of cells that can come back together if they are broken up by rocks tossed in the surf.

► The sea spider is not a true spider, but one of a group of related animals with eight to 12 sturdy legs and a tiny body. It feeds on anemones and similar animals.

The velvet swimming crab, which has red eyes, is occasionally found in rock pools and has flattened, paddle-like back legs that are adapted for swimming.

large numbers. This green or dull greyish species is distinguished by its inability to fully retract its purple-ended tentacles, so it cannot survive out of the water. Rock pools at the lower end of the shore are home to the dahlia anemone, a beautiful animal that prefers to cling to the angle between two rocks, and cover itself with gravel from the pool floor.

Encrusting algae

The sides of a rock pool are seldom just bare rock. Many organisms compete for hard surfaces on which to settle. Where there are no limpets, barnacles or anemones there will be various encrusting

organisms, including plant-like algae. Calcareous algae secrete chalky skeletons, either like a veneer over the rock surface, or in tufts, so they resemble corals. One of these algae forms a pink or mauve chalky crust that spreads to line rock pools. It is honeycombed with cavities that conceal tiny animals. Quite often this seaweed also encrusts the shells of larger animals, in particular those of limpets, so that at first glance it is not easy to spot the limpet until you notice the telltale gap around the shell's rim. The weed does not impede the limpet in any way and may even help to conceal it from predatory birds such as gulls.

Tufted coralline algae are also a common feature of rock pools. Their fronds are often used by shore-fish, such as the corkwing wrasse and the 15-spined stickleback, to make nests for their eggs. In sheltered places tufted corallines grow slender and elegant, but where conditions are rougher they are more stunted. Like encrusting algae, they may harbour many other organisms – around 2500 individuals for every gram of their dry weight – so they offer a real service to the small inhabitants of the pools.

Simple sponges

Sponges also spread their soft bodies over the pool sides. They can look rather like pieces of sodden bread, which explains why the commonest species is known as the breadcrumb sponge. These animals draw water through

Moulting crabs

Like other crustaceans, crabs can grow only by shedding their old shells and inflating their bodies to a larger size before they harden again. Sometimes newly moulted soft-bodied crabs can be found hiding in rock pools.

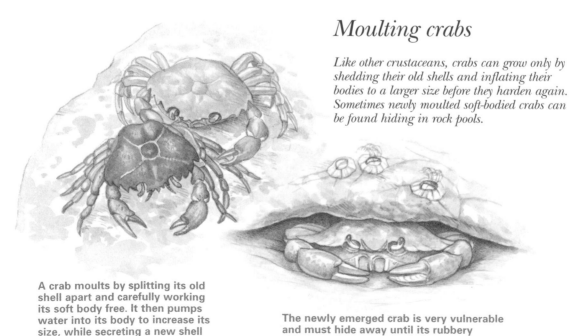

A crab moults by splitting its old shell apart and carefully working its soft body free. It then pumps water into its body to increase its size, while secreting a new shell that hardens within a few hours.

The newly emerged crab is very vulnerable and must hide away until its rubbery skin turns into a tough shell.

tiny holes and pump it around their bodies through canals and chambers. They extract food and oxygen from the water, then eject it through larger holes. The system may be simple, but it is highly effective, and sponges are among the most successful of all rock-pool animals. This success is partly explained by the way sponges possess a loose skeleton made of protein, chalk or silica, which makes them distasteful to other animals. The protein meshwork of a deep-sea sponge, when deprived of its living tissues, becomes a soft, absorbent bath sponge.

Natural aquarium

Insects do not generally frequent rock pools, but an insect-like creature, the wingless *Anurida maritima* (it has no common name), can be spotted in large swarms floating on the water's surface. These terrestrial animals are able to survive when the tide rises because rock pools always have crevices containing trapped bubbles of air. The insects locate these air pockets when flooding is imminent, and take refuge in them until the tide ebbs again.

Crabs and shrimps are common in rock pools, as are amphipods (sideways-flattened, woodlouse-like animals) and isopods (similar but flattened top to bottom). Tough external skeletons protect these crustaceans from waves and other hazards, and some species, such as the green shore crab, forage on dry rock as well as under the water.

The receding tide often strands inshore fish such as blennies and gobies. Blennies have a continuous dorsal fin, while gobies have a divided one. Gobies also have pelvic fins that form a sucker on the underside, which they use to withstand the swirl of water when the incoming tide floods the pool. Other stranded animals may include the young of larger fish, starfish, jellyfish, sea spiders, and sometimes an octopus.

Rock pools change with every tide, and no two are ever the same, so they provide an opportunity to study a limitless variety of marine life.

WHY ARE ALL ROCK POOLS DIFFERENT?

Rock-pool life varies according to the pool's position on the shore. For some species, the chief influence is the degree of exposure; for others, shelter from the sun is important. The dominant factor, however, is the pool's position relative to tidal rise and fall.

The combined attraction of moon and sun causes two oceanic surges to flow around the world. These tides arrive at any one place on average 50 minutes later each day. Normally, there are two periods of low tide and two of high tide in about 25 hours. Roughly 12 hours and 25 minutes separate each low tide, so they occur at a different time each day. On some days low tide occurs during the middle part of the day when the sun may be hot, and on other days it occurs in the cool of the morning or evening, when rock pools are less likely to heat up or dry out.

The moon takes 28 days to circle the earth, so the tides in any one place change every day on a 28-day cycle. When the moon is aligned with the sun this results in especially high and low spring tides every 14 days – the term referring not to the season but to the rise and fall of water.

Since the earth moves around the sun in an ellipse, there are two periods each year, in March and September, when the gravitational pull of the sun is at its greatest, causing spectacularly high and low tides called equinoctials.

All these tidal phenomena have a profound effect on the nature of rock pools and the shore life that inhabits them. The pattern of flooding and draining determines what sort of animals can survive in the pools, and since the pattern is always changing, the types of animals found in any one pool are always changing too.

Common starfish stranded by the outgoing tide will creep across the rock surface on hundreds of sucker-like tube feet until they are submerged again. Brief exposure does not harm them directly, but while they are in the open they are vulnerable to attack by scavenging gulls.

WILDLIFE WATCH

How can I explore rock pools safely?

Rock pools can be found on many coasts, especially on rocky northern and western shores, but before exploring them there are a few essential things to remember:

● Start back up the shore almost immediately after low water – it is easy to be caught unawares by a rising tide.

● Check the tide times, from tide tables or the local press. Aim to arrive on the shore one or two hours before predicted low water, and follow the tide down as it falls.

● Never run across a rocky shore – the rocks can be unstable and seaweeds can make them very slippery.

● Take a simple guide to shore-life and perhaps a camera, but do not take anything away except empty shells.

● Always replace any rocks and stones that are moved or turned over; otherwise prolonged exposure to the air will kill most of the organisms that have settled under them.

Coastal heath

When spring comes to maritime heathland, adders bask in the sun on open patches of grass, butterflies flit among the flowering heather and gorse, and the scolding calls of stonechats punctuate the salty air.

The coastal footpaths that thread their way along cliff edges around many of Britain's shores often pass through tracts of wild country that are dominated by low scrub and stunning displays of maritime flowers, especially in spring when thrift and sea campion are in bloom. These coastal roughlands are often based on hard rocks or free-draining sands and gravels that yield few nutrients to the soil. This encourages heather, gorse and other plants that thrive on acidic, nutrient-poor soil. Since this type of vegetation is usually associated with lowland heaths, these clifftop habitats are known as coastal or maritime heaths.

The evolution of lowland heath is inextricably linked to human activity. Much of the heathland that survives today would have been forested following the retreat of the glaciers at the end of the last Ice Age, but as people colonised the land they gradually cleared it to provide pasture for their animals. The combination of grazing pressure and regular, controlled burning – to promote fresh plant growth for grazing – prevented the regrowth of trees, and over the centuries the exposed, thin soils had their nutrients washed out of them by the rain. The result was a landscape dominated by heather, which is one of the few plants that can thrive on such soils. This is the origin of the word 'heath'.

Unique habitats

Several heaths that developed in this way occur near the coast, but there is evidence that true coastal or maritime heaths had rather different origins. Such heathlands are distinguished by a unique combination of plants, which seems to have evolved as a result of natural factors rather than deliberate land clearance.

This is particularly true of some of the coastal heaths found on many parts of the Cornish coast, on the Isles of Scilly and in Pembrokeshire in south Wales. These heaths may be what is known as a 'climax community' – a term given to the final stage of natural plant colonisation of any piece of land. In this process the habitat evolves through a succession of different phases, each with its own dominant type of vegetation, unless it is prevented from doing so by some inhibiting factor such as intensive grazing. Over most of Britain – including places that are now lowland heaths – the final phase tends to be forest. By contrast, coastal heaths have developed in

The noisy, inquisitive stonechat is a conspicuous breeding bird of coastal heaths. The showy males often perch prominently on sprays of gorse.

▲ Foxes regularly hunt over tracts of coastal heath, targeting the many rabbits and voles that feed on and among the grasses and heathers.

▶ Cliff-top plants, such as thrift and rock sea lavender, also thrive on the sandy heathland found at the back of a beach.

◀ Western gorse, which is much scarcer than common gorse, has bright yellow flowers and can flourish on coastal heaths, especially in the west.

▶ Spring squill prefers coastal heaths and grassland to inland sites. A diminutive relative of the bluebell, it has bright violet-blue blooms.

▶ The gorse shield bug is often found on sprays of gorse where it uses its sharp, needle-like mouthparts to pierce the plant and drink its sap.

▶ Attracted by gorse, on which the female lays her eggs, the green hairstreak butterfly thrives on many coastal heaths.

areas where the soil type favours heathland plants, but where the action of wind and salty sea spray prevents the final stage of colonisation by trees. The natural 'pruning' effect of the salty wind also helps restrict the heathers and other shrubs to a height that seldom exceeds knee-level, and they often take the form of low, rounded hummocks.

On any stretch of coastal heathland the plant life is usually dominated by three species – ling (also known simply as heather), bell heather and western gorse. The plants may grow in a mosaic of single-species patches, or all mixed together with heather shoots of both species appearing through a spiny, tangled blanket of intertwining gorse stems. Other typical plants of coastal heathland include common gorse, bracken and sheep's fescue grass, while the maritime influence is evident from the presence of spring squill, as well as several plants of sea cliffs, such as thrift, sea plantain and buck's-horn plantain.

As with other heathland habitats, the ground often supports lichens, including several colourful species of *Cladonia*, as well as the strange and distinctive

▲ The Lizard peninsula has a unique species of coastal heath dominated by heather called Cornish heath – a plant that is unknown elsewhere in Britain.

▲ Dense vegetation provides cover for the pygmy shrew, which is able to forage for food without being seen by predatory birds.

Teloschistes flavicans. This coastal lichen stands out both because of its curious appearance – it resembles a tangle of orange thread-like worms writhing on the ground – and its very restricted distribution. It is found only on the coastal heaths of the south-west.

◄ The Lapland bunting is an occasional visitor to coastal heathland, pausing on its journey between the Arctic and wintering quarters in Europe.

▼ Stone walls act like rocky outcrops, enabling widespread coastal plants such as thrift to grow without competing with the heather.

Heath insects

The mild, frost-free climate of maritime heaths suits insects that can tolerate the salt spray and strong winds. In spring, oil beetles and dor beetles can often be seen crawling among the vegetation, and green tiger beetles frequently take to the air between the areas of bare ground where they hunt for other insects. Other small predators include the heath assassin bug, as well as several species of hunting and web-spinning spiders.

► From early April, a green tiger beetle may be seen scurrying over bare ground in search of insect prey, or flying up with a flash of its bluish abdomen.

Butterflies can often be found in great numbers on calm days in spring and early summer. Those found only on heathland include graylings, small heaths, silver-studded blues and green hairstreaks, while widespread species, such as small whites, often pause on the heath to feed as they pass through on migration. Moths such as the day-flying emperor moth, the nocturnal true lover's knot and the beautiful yellow underwing may emerge from their cocoons, hidden among heathland plants.

Despite the low-growing nature of the vegetation, the larger animals of coastal heaths are by no means easy

▶ Common lizards bask among the vegetation on convenient tree stumps or wooden posts, slipping away into cover when they sense danger.

▲ Migrant wheatears pass through in March and April and again in autumn. Some remain all summer to breed.

to see. Early spring is the best time to look for the adders and common lizards that live among the heather. Both are numerous where they occur, and are most likely to be seen basking in the open after awakening from hibernation. Small mammals, including pygmy shrews and field voles, are mostly nocturnal, and even the rabbits are cautious, rarely emerging from their burrows until late afternoon, and always keeping a lookout for passing foxes.

Visiting birds
One of the most characteristic coastal heathland birds is the stonechat. Throughout spring and summer these flamboyant little birds scold intruders with their 'sweet tchack tchack' calls, the last two notes sounding like two pebbles knocked together. Far less conspicuous

▲ Unspoilt areas of coastal heath often support thriving populations of silver-studded blues. These butterflies fly from late June to mid-August.

are the Dartford warblers, despite the fact that coastal heaths harbour the largest populations of this species in Britain. These tiny, long-tailed, grey and wine-red birds tend to skulk in gorse bushes, and are more often heard than seen. The males produce a scratchy but musical warbling song, which they often deliver from the top of a gorse bush before disappearing into cover once more. Both sexes have a buzzing 'tchurr' call.

On spring mornings, warm patches of ground are often claimed by adders, sunning themselves before a day's hunting.

▶ *Teloschistes flavicans* is a distinctive, scarce lichen that is often found on rocks or bare ground on coastal heaths, mainly in south-west England.

More because of its seaside location than the nature of the habitat, coastal heath is a good place to see migrant songbirds in spring. Wheatears are often the first to arrive, with far more birds being seen in transit than actually breed.

WILDLIFE WATCH

Where can I visit coastal heath?

Coastal heathland is largely confined to south-western Britain. However, isolated examples of the habitat can be found in parts of Wales, Suffolk and a few other places around the coast.

1 Isles of Scilly
Subject to a mild, oceanic climate, these windswept islands off Cornwall have pockets of coastal heath around their margins. Good spots include Peninnis Head on St Mary's, and the southern reaches of Tresco and St Agnes.

2 Cornwall
The Lizard peninsula harbours many rare and unusual plants. The best areas of heath are found around Kynance Cove. The coastal footpath north from Land's End also has large tracts of heath, which are important staging posts for migrant birds. On the north coast, visit St Agnes Head and Chapel Porth for some splendid stretches of heath and stunning views.

3 North Devon
Many parts of the Exmoor coast are covered in well-developed coastal heath. Countisbury Point in the northern quarter of Lundy island also harbours some pockets of coastal heath.

4 West Wales
The Pembrokeshire coastal path passes through some prime areas of coastal heath; one of the best sites is Strumble Head.

5 North Wales
North Wales also has some areas of coastal heath. The best sites are South Stack on Anglesey and near the tip of the Lleyn peninsula.

The Wye valley

Steep-sided gorges and undulating plains line the Wye valley as the river winds its way towards the sea, where woodland banks are replaced by gleaming mudflats and bird-rich salt marshes.

Lying on the border between England and Wales, just north of the Severn estuary, the Wye valley is one of the most varied and spectacular landscapes in lowland Britain. Rising high in mid-Wales, the Wye flows through mountainous terrain until, near Hereford, it glides into flatter regions. Above Goodrich, the river swings in grand curves across a wide plain, with gently rolling country to either side. Downstream of Goodrich, however, the scene changes dramatically as the river cuts through 100m (330ft) deep gorges and loops round the base of the 200m (660ft) high Symond's Yat rock, famous for its nesting peregrines. Below Monmouth the river flows through a deeply incised valley to its estuary below Chepstow, skirting grand limestone crags at Tintern and Wyndcliff.

The Wye valley has been a popular tourist attraction since the 18th century. Visitors would board a boat in Ross and drift downstream to Monmouth, where they had the option of extending their journey to Tintern. There they could view the picturesque ruins of the Cistercian abbey, the subject of many romantic paintings and a famous poem by William Wordsworth. Indeed, the ruins survive in such an impressive form partly because their owners, the Dukes of Beaufort, were quick to recognise their appeal and took pains to preserve them. Many of today's visitors choose to follow the Wye Valley Walk, a well-signposted route between Hereford and Chepstow that includes many of the finest sights.

Salmon river

The Wye is one of the cleanest of Britain's major waterways, a fact reflected in the number of aquatic plants and animals it supports. It is a thriving salmon river, something that is comparatively rare nowadays in lowland Britain. Salmon require different conditions

◀ Having escaped serious pollution, the Wye supports a healthy salmon population. The fish spawn in the shallow upper reaches, then move downriver to feed and grow.

and stone loaches, which favour the sheltered margins and backwaters, to open-water species including bream, perch, dace and chub. The fish stocks are plentiful enough to support a healthy population of otters, plus several species of fish-eating birds, such as kingfishers and grey herons, and in winter, goosanders and cormorants.

Aquatic insects

Such thriving populations of fish, in particular, could not survive without a variety of aquatic invertebrates on which to feed. The clear, nutrient-rich waters harbour a wealth

One of the club-tailed dragonfly's British strongholds is the River Wye. On spring mornings, newly emerged yellow and black adults cling to the stems of waterside plants.

for different stages in their life cycle, and the Wye provides all of them. Its upper reaches offer clear, gravelly shallows for spawning, while farther downstream plenty of deeper sections allow the young fish – or 'parr' – to feed and grow.

Salmon are not the only fish found in the Wye. Others range in size from minnows

At 250km (155 miles), the Wye is one of the longest rivers in England and Wales, and the whole valley has Site of Special Scientific Interest status.

OTTER AND MINK

The clean waters of the Wye are well stocked with fish, which is one reason why that most elusive of British mammals, the otter, is numerous in the Wye valley. It is one of few sites in southern Britain where otters continued to live when habitat loss and persecution drove them to extinction elsewhere, and their numbers have increased in recent years.

As always, otters here are difficult to watch, but they often leave conspicuous signs. Look for mud chutes down steep banks, and sticky black droppings – known as spraints – conspicuously placed on rocks or tree

stumps. The chances of seeing otters increase upstream and in quieter stretches of the river, away from houses and car parks.

Identifying an otter is not always straightforward, however. Many apparent sightings of otters are in fact glimpses of American mink, which having escaped from captivity are now breeding in the region. While the otter recovery is welcomed by naturalists, and tolerated by the authorities who manage the river for fishing, the increasing population of mink is a cause for concern, because these voracious hunters threaten native species, such as water voles.

◀ The American mink can be distinguished from the otter by its smaller size, more pointed snout, darker colouring, and lack of pale fur on the chest. Also, it swims with the whole of its back and head exposed whereas when an otter is swimming, its head is all that is visible.

▼ Although it is more elusive than the mink, an otter may sometimes be seen in the open. However, it rarely strays far from water.

PEREGRINES AT SYMOND'S YAT

The imposing cliffs at Symond's Yat – an old name for 'gap' or 'pass' – offer superb views over the river and surrounding area, including the nearby Forest of Dean. The view in itself is a big draw for visitors, but for the birdwatcher there is an added bonus – the opportunity to watch breeding peregrine falcons.

These magnificent birds of prey can often be seen flying over the forest as they commute to their estuarine hunting grounds to the south. At Symond's Yat, however, a pair nest in full view. With the aid of telescopes provided by the RSPB, who manage the viewpoint, it is possible to see intimate details of the day-to-day life of a peregrine pair and their ever-hungry offspring.

Early spring is the best time of year to visit the site. If the day is warm and sunny there is a good chance of seeing the pair performing their aerial displays, and even passing food to one another in mid-air if nesting itself has not commenced. Thereafter, the birds become a lot more retiring in their habits, with one bird – usually the female – sitting on the eggs while the other stands guard on a rock ledge nearby.

Once the young have hatched – usually mid-May to mid-June – there is another burst of activity, with both birds spending a good deal of their time hunting for prey and returning to the nest to feed the chicks. A few weeks later, the newly fledged young take to the wing, the whole family party becoming extremely vocal. The adults can be seen teaching their offspring to catch prey in flight.

Like most peregrine nests in Britain, the nest at Symond's Yat is guarded by dedicated observers to prevent anyone stealing the eggs or young birds to supply the lucrative falconry trade, as occurred in 1983. Announcing the location publicly in 1984 had an unexpected benefit, since the constant presence of birdwatchers has made the site almost self-policing. There is seldom a moment when the nest is not being scrutinised through telescopes or binoculars, making the covert removal of eggs or young very difficult.

of underwater life, including pollution-sensitive mayflies and stoneflies. The Wye is particularly well known for its club-tailed dragonflies. These nationally scarce insects are best looked for as they emerge from their larval stage – between mid-May and late June in this area – when adult dragonflies can sometimes be found in the early morning resting on waterside vegetation. By late morning most of the newly emerged dragonflies have flown, leaving only their empty cocoons still attached to plant stems.

Blue flash
The healthy state of the Wye is also reflected in the bird life encountered along its banks. Overhanging branches with dappled foliage provide ideal perches for kingfishers which, despite their bright plumage, are often remarkably hard to see against the leaves. Sooner or later, however, one will break cover and fly low over the water, the electric blue feathers on its back flashing in the spring sunlight. It may even be seen diving after a fish and, if successful, returning to its perch with its catch.

Both peregrine parents feed the young, regularly returning to the nest site with prey, such as pigeons. They tear the food into bite-sized morsels before offering it to the downy nestlings.

Where the river is broad and shallow in its upper reaches, it is a paradise for salmon, trout and otters, while the fringing woodland contains many species of birds, such as sparrowhawks and woodcocks.

▲ A dipper rests between underwater foraging expeditions, perching on a midstream boulder in a stony stretch of the river.

▲ Loud, sharp, high 'tsick' calls announce the presence of a grey wagtail pair on the river. The birds often nest under bridges.

► An exposed sandy bank is an ideal nest site for sand martins. These birds excavate burrows using their tiny bill and claws.

Steep, eroded banks along the Wye provide ideal sites for kingfishers to excavate nesting burrows. Such places are also used by the sand martins that arrive each spring to nest in colonies. Like their relatives the swallows and house martins, sand martins are insect feeders that specialise in catching their prey on the wing, often hawking low over the water. Other aerial insect feeders are common here, too, especially on warm spring evenings when parties of swifts join forces with the martins and swallows to feast on the midges and other insects swarming over the water.

Like many other rivers in the region, the Wye supports flourishing populations of grey wagtails and dippers. During the breeeding season both are often associated with man-made structures. Dippers and grey wagtails frequently breed under bridges, and grey wagtails also nest in gaps in old stone walls, or among loose brickwork and stones in waterside buildings.

Throughout the year, both species are to be seen perched on stones and boulders in mid-water. Grey wagtails make aerial sorties after insects from these vantage points, while dippers plunge under water in search of aquatic insect larvae, walking upstream over the river bed beneath the fast-flowing current.

Flowers and woods
The banks of the lower Wye are heavily wooded, but here and there, where wet meadows lie alongside the flowing water, the banks support a rich marginal flora of water avens, ragged robin, lesser spearwort and meadowsweet. In many places the shallows near the river margin are carpeted with long, flexing trails of flowering water-crowfoot, which is at its best in late spring.

The woodland that shades the banks of the river is very varied, and a typical area might include a mixture of lime, oak, beech, ash and wych elm, largely preserved by the traditional coppicing that provided fuel for the local iron and tin workings in the past. The limestone cliffs are marked by groves of yew growing among the beech, together with some rare local forms of whitebeam. Ancient woodland species such as

▲ In early spring, although deciduous trees are still almost leafless, drifts of spring flowers, such as these wood anemones, bloom on the sunlit forest floor.

◄ Bluebells growing on a grassy slope among rocks are a sign that the site was once wooded. In spring many woods flanking the river are filled with bluebells.

► During the summer months, the bright yellow blooms of Welsh poppy are a common sight on moist, shady banks along the Wye valley.

wild service tree and small-leaved lime complete the picture, with clouds of white wild cherry blossom in spring. Many of the trees are draped with lichens and mosses, providing refuges and food for large numbers of insects.

In spring these woods are excellent places to look for pied flycatchers. These birds have benefited greatly from the provision of nestboxes. Pied flycatchers can be detected by their simple, sweet, warbling song, often accompanied by the shivering trills of wood warblers high above in the tall beeches and oaks. Both are spring visitors, as is the tree pipit, which performs its conspicuous song-flights over the trees, flying up silently from a branch and then parachuting down while uttering its loud, sweet, trilling song. The shy redstart can also be seen here, flickering its distinctive brick-coloured tail, and the woods are a good place to watch woodpeckers. All three British species – the green, great spotted and lesser spotted – inhabit them throughout the year.

Bats are well represented along the wooded margins of the river, for some of the region's largest colonies of lesser and greater horseshoe bats are located nearby. Visiting breeding or hibernation sites would cause too much disturbance for the bats, but an evening stroll along the river is often rewarded by the thrilling sight of hunting bats swooping low over the water where the air is thick with insects.

Tidal reaches

Below Bigsweir the river becomes tidal, and the influence of salt water is marked by a change in the vegetation. Estuarine species such as glasswort become increasingly common, as do other salt marsh plants that replace freshwater species.

The Wye joins the Severn close to the old Severn road bridge. Crossing the bridge at low tide it is possible to see the extent of the mudflats and their fringing salt marshes. Nearer the mouth, the exposed shore at low tide offers feeding opportunities for various species of waders. Flocks of dunlin will be much in evidence in spring, along with ringed plovers and smaller numbers of grey plovers, knot, sanderling and whimbrel. Later in the year they are joined by curlews, redshanks and lapwings.

Quite unlike the wooded country upriver, these saltings at the edge of the land mark the end of the Wye river valley.

In autumn the leaves of oaks and many other deciduous trees turn the slopes of the river valley a glorious golden brown for a few short weeks.

Places to visit in the Wye valley

Few other areas of the Welsh border country, and indeed Britain, can offer such glorious scenery, but as well as dramatic landscapes, the Wye valley region has plenty to attract lovers of wildlife throughout the year.

1 Lugg Meadows near Hereford is a nature reserve run by the Herefordshire Nature Trust. It is a good spot to look for club-tailed dragonflies, which also occur farther downriver. The meadows after which the site is named are full of damp-loving flowers, including ragged robin, cuckooflower, great burnet and the very rare snake's-head fritillary.

2 Symond's Yat is renowned for its nesting peregrines and superb views of the Wye valley, but the woodlands are also well worth exploring. In spring the flowers include herb-Paris and early purple orchid, while nesting birds include local specialities such as redstarts and pied flycatchers.

3 Highbury Wood near Monmouth, lies on the path of Offa's Dyke, a boundary between England and Wales created at the time of the Saxon king Offa. It is a limestone woodland protected by National Nature Reserve status. Like Lady Park Wood, also near Monmouth, but just south of Symond's Yat, it has a range of interesting woodland flowers including spurge-laurel, herb-Paris, bird's-nest orchid, woodruff, small-leaved lime, large-leaved lime, whitebeam and wild service tree. Birdlife includes summer visiting wood warblers, pied flycatchers and redstarts, along with resident woodpeckers and buzzards.

4 Between Tintern and Chepstow lies some spectacular scenery and superb woodland. Footpaths follow the course of the river from Brockweir southward. The lowest section is truly stunning with a deep, eroded gorge at its heart. The wooded slopes nearer to Tintern are full of interesting flowers such as upright or Tintern spurge – a local speciality – herb-Paris, lesser calamint, giant bellflower, common wintergreen and marjoram. Butterflies are particularly prevalent here, with silver-washed and small pearl-bordered fritillaries, speckled wood and holly blue. Birds include all the woodland species typical of the region such as nuthatch, little owl, wood warbler, pied flycatcher and redstart.

Miles 0   4   8   12
Km 0   5   10   15   20

LEOMINSTER
R. Wigg
R. Wye
HEREFORD
1 LUGG MEADOWS
WYE VALLEY
SELLACK COMMON
ROSS-ON-WYE
R. Monnow
GOODRICH CASTLE
2 SYMOND'S YAT
HIGHMEADOW WOODS
MONMOUTH
COLEFORD
FOREST OF DEAN
HIGHBURY WOOD **3**
HEWELSFIELD COMMON
TINTERN
BROCKWEIR
4
CHEPSTOW
N

WILDLIFE WATCH

What can I see in the Wye valley?

● For woodland flowers, the best time to visit is in spring, preferably between late April and early June. Recently coppiced areas with plenty of open clearings offer the best variety of plants.

● Resident woodland birds are easiest to see from late March when the chorus of singing male birds fills the air. Migrants such as pied flycatchers and redstarts arrive from mid-April.

● The peregrines at Symond's Yat are best seen in early spring when the adults are displaying, or in early summer when the young take to the wing. The RSPB/Forest Enterprise peregrine viewing point is open from 10am every day from early April to the end of August. Telephone the RSPB on 01767 680551, or visit enquiries@rspb.org.uk for more information.

Although herb-Paris has a very patchy distribution nationally, it is common in some woodlands in the Wye valley region, especially where the woods are still regularly coppiced.

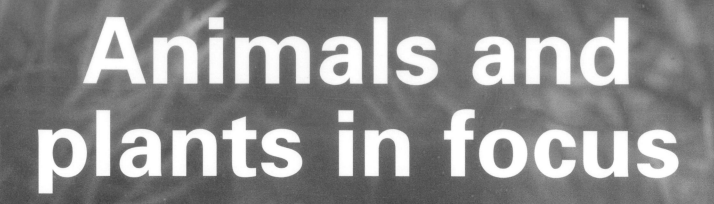

Animals and plants in focus

Waterside watch

- The mink
- The grey heron
- Recognising swifts and swallows
- The osprey
- The pike
- The stickleback
- The smooth newt
- Recognising frogs and toads
- Mayflies
- Aquatic plants

The mink

A waterside animal, the mink hunts most actively at night. With its long, athletic body, this carnivore is an excellent climber and swimmer and catches its prey on land and in water.

The mink is the first undomesticated carnivore from another country known to have adapted successfully to living wild in the British Isles. Resident for only the last few decades, the mink was first imported in 1929 from America by British fur farmers. Mink bred well in captivity and could be fed cheaply on unwanted animal waste produced, for example, by poultry farms.

The mink's fur is shiny and soft, and it also has a dense and fluffy underfur that protects it from cold when swimming. This underfur can be made into expensive coats and trimmings. Careful selection of animals for breeding allowed mink to be produced with different-coloured furs, ranging from silver-white to cream, as well as the natural dark chocolate brown. The pale – called 'pastel' – mink furs fetched an especially high price.

Escaping into the wild

The mink industry expanded rapidly during the 1950s with the importing of large numbers of animals – often as many as 700 in a single shipment – from North America. By 1962 there were more than 700 mink farms in Britain, producing 160,000 pelts per year, a figure that quickly rose to more than a quarter of a million.

With so many animals being kept, often in poorly secured cages, it was inevitable that escapes would occur. Mink are athletic animals, able to climb well, and they also proved adept at squeezing through surprisingly small gaps. Those that escaped adapted well to living in the wild and, with farms scattered all over the country, right from the outset, mink began to colonise many areas of Britain and Ireland. The first confirmed reports of mink breeding in the wild came from Devon in the late 1950s. In the 1960s, the Ministry of Agriculture began a trapping campaign to eliminate them but despite the killing of a thousand or more each year – in addition to those trapped or shot by gamekeepers – the population continued to expand.

The mink has a distinctive pale patch of fur stretching from its chin to its throat. The mink prefers to inhabit wooded areas near water where it hunts a wide variety of prey.

MINK FACT FILE

The mink is a small, lithe mammal, with the long body and short legs typical of the family that includes otters, weasels, skunks and badgers. With a covering of shiny guard hairs over thick underfur, and slightly webbed feet, the mink is well adapted for its waterside lifestyle.

● **NAMES**
Common name: American mink, mink
Scientific name: *Mustela vison*

● **HABITAT**
Mostly lowland areas, beside rivers, lakes and ponds

● **DISTRIBUTION**
Almost everywhere in mainland Britain; absent from Isle of Wight, Isle of Man and Anglesey; absent from extreme north of Scotland but present on Lewis and Arran

● **STATUS**
Around 36,000; major decline since 1995

● **SIZE**
Length head and body 30–45cm (12–18in), tail 13–23cm (5–9in); weight adult females about 450–800g (16–28oz), males 850–1800g (30–63½oz)

● **KEY FEATURES**
Coat chocolate brown to black with pale markings on chin, throat and underside; silver blue or pale brown mutations, feet slightly webbed

● **HABITS**
Active day and night, but mostly in the evening and after dark; lives near water

● **VOICE**
Purrs when mating; hisses when threatened; may shriek in self-defence, but usually silent

● **FOOD**
Fish, frogs, small mammals, waterside birds and their eggs; some invertebrates; raids fish farms and captive waterfowl

● **BREEDING**
One litter per year, in April or May; usually 4–7 young per litter; weaning period is 5–6 weeks

● **NEST**
Uses burrows and lairs among tree roots at water's edge, also rabbit burrows; rarely digs its own burrows

● **YOUNG**
Resemble adult, but smaller

● **SIGNS**
Footprints in soft mud show pad and often only 4 of the 5 toes in a splayed-out star shape, 2.5–4cm (1–1½in) long and 2–4cm (¾–1½in) wide; droppings tapered at each end, about 5–8cm (2–3in) long, typically 1cm (½in) diameter, deposited on waterside objects such as stones and logs, unpleasantly smelly

All wild mink in Britain are descended from animals that escaped from fur farms. Today, a few are still born with the silver-blue or pale-brown fur that was developed in captivity. These individuals are known as pastel mink.

Distribution map key

▮ Present all year round

☐ Not present

MINK AND THE LAW
The Mink (Importation and Keeping) Order, banning the importation of American mink, was passed in 1962 under the Destructive Imported Animals Act of 1932.

Small, rounded ears are almost hidden in fur.

The neck is thick and muscular, the body slender and sinuous.

Dense, glossy fur is moulted twice in a year.

Slightly bushy, the tail is approximately half the length of the body.

By 1971, mink were found in 41 counties in England and Wales, with many also living in different parts of Scotland and Ireland. Their spread into eastern England was slow but they are now common there, too. In less than half a century, the mink became one of Britain's most prevalent carnivores. A 1995 estimate showed a population of about 110,000, making the mink far more numerous than either the otter or the polecat. Since then, however, there has been a massive decline in the mink population. In 2004 it was estimated at about 37,000 – a result, perhaps, of the increase in otters which occupy the same waterside territory.

New predator

Much controversy surrounded the mink's successful adaptation to living wild in Britain. At first, it was thought to be occupying an 'ecological vacancy'. Europe is home to the European mink, which has never lived in Britain. It was claimed that

▼ With their long bodies and alert posture, mink are occasionally confused with otters, which also live on the waterside. However, mink are smaller and slimmer, and darker in colour with a more pointed snout.

▲ Despite the mink's notoriety for hunting waterfowl and game fish, rabbits are one of its favourite foods. In some areas, rabbits form the majority of the mink's diet. It also hunts smaller animals, such as voles.

the American mink was filling this gap, being intermediate in size between the larger otter and smaller stoat. It was also seen as a replacement for the polecat, which had been exterminated over much of Britain – although polecat numbers are now increasing.

However, while a few mink would have had little effect on Britain's wildlife, tens of thousands of this carnivorous animal resulted in the destruction of large numbers of other animals. Mink got into zoos and parks with captive ducks – often with clipped wings so that they could not fly – and killed many birds. They also created havoc on chicken and fish farms, where they found plenty to eat but carried on killing even when they were no longer hungry. Gamekeepers soon added mink to their list of vermin.

Mink and other wildlife

Soon public opinion began to swing against the mink as an unwelcome addition to British wildlife and it was blamed for ousting another fish-eating animal, the otter. However, studies show that there is little competition between the animals for food – mink eat fish that are too small for otters to bother with, and many other types of prey that are unimportant to otters. Recent research suggests that otters have had a direct impact on the far smaller mink by driving them away and sometimes even killing them. Where otters are increasing, mink numbers tend to decline – dramatically so where otters have been reintroduced and their densities are particularly high.

Mink have, however, had a severe effect on water vole populations. Water voles, like mink, live alongside rivers and lakes, but they are slow swimmers and easy for mink to catch in the water.

Once mink occupied a new area, water vole numbers there declined. Within two or three years of the first mink being spotted, water voles often disappeared completely. Although the water vole is no longer present in more than 80 per cent of the sites it inhabited before the arrival of mink, other reasons have contributed to its decline – most particularly destruction of the river banks where it lives. This is now being rectified and water voles reintroduced to some areas.

Other inhabitants of the waterside, such as moorhens and coots, are also easily captured by mink, and in some places it has significantly reduced the numbers of ducks and other waterfowl.

Island invaders

Strong swimmers, mink can easily get to small islands where birds nest out of the reach of foxes, cats and stoats. Colonies of gulls, terns and waders have been severely affected by mink invading their previously secure homes. In the sheltered waters of Scottish lochs, mink can swim as far as islands more than 3km (1¾ miles) offshore. There they may kill hundreds of adult birds and growing chicks, as well as eating the eggs. Entire colonies of seabirds have been destroyed in the space of just a few breeding seasons. In some parts of western Scotland, seabird numbers have been halved by mink.

These areas previously offered seabirds a haven in which they became particularly numerous, so it might be argued that the

mink has only reduced their numbers to a more 'natural' level. Whatever opinions might be held about the mink, it is here to stay. No amount of shooting and trapping is likely to eradicate it now. This successful predator has become an established and familiar part of Britain's wetlands.

Solitary hunter

Much smaller than the otter, mink are about 35cm (14in) long with a bushy tail. Their distinctive silky fur is much darker than that of the otter. When wet, they appear almost black whereas otters are clearly brown. The mink's droppings, which are deposited on rocks and logs at the water's edge, are easily recognisable,

A splashing doggy-paddle allows the mink to cross rivers, but to catch prey it must swim quietly underwater. A layer of dense underfur protects it against cold water in winter. Mink may even swim beneath ice.

being thin, black and cylindrical. They smell acrid, while those of the otter have a musky but not unpleasant odour.

Mink most often live near slow-flowing rivers and lowland lakes and are less common in upland areas. In some places, particularly in Scotland, they live along the seashore. They have formed colonies in some coastal areas where there may be as many as two mink per kilometre (just over half a mile) of rocky coast. Along the seashore, mink behave

Hunting high and low

Mink always remain close to water and frequent places with ample waterside vegetation. Even when roaming, they tend to follow streams and ditches. Mink eat a varied carnivorous diet, taking whatever prey is available to them on land and in water.

When hunting for fish, mink move stealthily along the bank, peering into the water. When they spot a fish, they dive in to pursue it. Only when the water is deep or the bank not easily negotiated will the mink hunt in a more otter-like manner, swimming in search of prey.

Mink are strong swimmers and competent predators in the water. They usually take slower moving prey, such as eels and crayfish, although they also have a taste for trout and salmon, which makes them unpopular with fishermen.

▲ Its slightly webbed toes allow the mink to swim so well. With a coating of long, shiny guard hairs, its wet fur looks spiky as the animal leaves the stream. The mink shakes off excess water and may sit on the bank to groom its coat.

◄ Mink are such successful hunters that they spend less than 20 per cent of their time away from their dens searching for prey. In the safety of their dens, they sleep or groom themselves.

▲ As a territorial animal, the male mink will not tolerate the proximity of a rival, although it is less aggressive towards females. Male and female territories are mainly separate, but occasionally overlap.

in a similar way to coastal otters, feeding on rock-pool fish, but they also climb steep, grassy cliff slopes to raid gulls' nests. They are particularly partial to the eggs of gulls and terns, which are narrower at one end and therefore easy to break into. Before breaking larger eggs, a mink may drag them to cover among long vegetation. If there is an excess of food, it is often stored to eat later.

Mink are not sociable and each one tends to live in its own waterside territory, which is usually about 2–3km (1¼–1¾ miles) in length but sometimes as much as 6km (3⅗ miles) long. Along rivers and shores, mink territories are mainly linear, although they are more irregular around marshland. Male territories do not overlap, but often include parts of the territories of one or more females.

Courtship and breeding

In spring, some males set out on long journeys in search of females and may travel many kilometres across the countryside, even away from rivers. There is no pair bond and, after mating, the animals separate. Females produce just one litter each year, usually in late April or May. The average litter size is four to seven, although it can be as much as 10. In captivity, mink sometimes produce up to 17 youngsters.

The young spend up to two months in their mother's nest, which is usually situated in a burrow or among waterside stones or dense tree roots. They are weaned at approximately five to six weeks old. From June onwards the young mink learn how to forage and hunt for food with their mother. The family disperses when the youngsters are about 13 to 14 weeks old, and they then grow rapidly to reach adult size before the end of the year. They are capable of breeding during the following year, by the time they are 10 to 11 months old. Females are still able to breed when they are as much as seven years old, although most mink in the wild die within the first three years of life. The oldest wild mink on record lived to be 10 years old.

Young mink tend to move away from their mother's territory after August, sometimes travelling more than 10km (6 miles) to find a new place to live. During their travels, weaker individuals

FREEING CAPTIVE MINK

In 1998, animal rights supporters broke into a number of fur farms and released several thousand mink into the wild. This act was widely condemned by conservationists and animal-welfare groups for two main reasons. Firstly, the released mink posed a serious threat to many other animals. For example, one of the fur-farm releases was in the New Forest. Here, rare reptiles and ground-nesting birds, such as the nightjar, were put at risk from the high numbers of mink set loose into the countryside. Under the Wildlife and Countryside Act, it is illegal to release animals that have not previously occupied an area into the wild due to the damage they are likely to do. This is especially true when large numbers are released into a single area.

Secondly, such releases are cruel to the mink themselves. The animals that originally escaped to form the population of wild mink in Britain were adventurous and adaptable creatures. However, many of the released mink had never been outside a cage before and were confused and disoriented. While some individuals no doubt learned to survive, many were easily recaptured, having never learnt the skills required to live independently of human beings. In a short time, large numbers were run over on the roads while others were killed by dogs or shot by landowners and gamekeepers. Some of the mink even found their way into people's houses, having been driven by hunger to enter via cat flaps in search of food. The majority of these freed mink were not able to fend for themselves in the wild.

Today's farmed mink have been bred in captivity for many generations. Unlike their more adaptable ancestors, they are mainly not able to succeed in the wild if they are released or escape.

▼ Mink produce one litter a year. The young are born in a den among waterside stones or tree roots. From June onwards each youngster can be seen learning how to forage with its mother.

are driven away if they stray on to territory that has already been claimed. Most mink that die from natural causes probably do so as a result of territorial disputes with other mink – they may die of starvation as a result of being driven out of areas where prey is most abundant. Once successful individuals have established a territory, they tend to remain in the same place, often for several years.

For its den, the mink may use an old rabbit burrow or a hiding place among rocks or even piles of brushwood. The den is rarely more than a distance of 10m (33ft) away from the water's edge and may sometimes have a separate entrance underwater. Each mink may use several dens at different times of the year, which are spread along its territory. Mink do not hibernate, although they become significantly less active during the cold winter months.

▲ Basking in the sun, a mink surveys its territory. This is usually a stretch of river bank or an area around the edge of a lake or marsh. Mink may also live along the seashore, where their prey includes crabs, molluscs and small fish.

The mink's diet consists mainly of fish and birds as well as other small animals, although they also attack larger animals, such as rabbits. Beetles, worms and other invertebrates are considered worth eating, but generally they will not eat plants.

Natural survivor

Otters have been known to kill mink, but mink are capable of defending themselves against attacks by foxes or cats. Mink have little to fear from most natural predators, which is perhaps why they are often active in broad daylight, although they mainly hunt after dark.

Human beings are the only significant threat. Mink are in constant danger from gamekeepers and farmers, and several thousand are shot or trapped each year. Others may drown in traps set to catch fish. Mink hunting with hounds – trained to track only mink – began in the late 1970s, with a season lasting from April until October. However, mink hunting has been banned under the Hunting with Dogs legislation.

WILDLIFE WATCH

Where can I see mink?

● The best places to look for mink are beside quiet, slow-flowing rivers, especially in Kent, Sussex, Devon and Pembrokeshire, where they have long been established in the wild.

● Select a suitable tree or bridge as a vantage point and watch quietly without moving. The best time to look is in the early evening.

● Asking local anglers where they see mink is one way to find a spot to watch for them. Another is to search under bridges and on boulders and logs for their characteristic droppings.

With a thick fur coat, the mink is well insulated against the worst of the winter weather. However, if rivers, lakes or marshes freeze, mink may be forced to travel farther afield in search of food.

The grey heron

Flying overhead with large, distinctively bowed wings and legs trailing behind its tail, the grey heron is a familiar sight. At the edge of rivers and lakes, it stands as still as a statue, waiting for its next meal.

A striking bird, the grey heron is almost 1m (3ft) tall with a wingspan of nearly 2m (6ft). Only a small number of British birds, such as swans, rare golden and white-tailed eagles and cranes, have wingspans equalling or exceeding this. For such a big bird, it flies easily, with its neck retracted and using lazy beats of its big, broad wings.

The grey heron is one of the few heron species – the others are the little egret and the bittern – to breed regularly as far north as the British Isles, and some nest as far north as the west coast of Norway. Herons nest together in colonies, called 'heronries', but they are generally solitary feeders. This suits their main hunting method, which is to stand motionless in, or move very slowly through, shallow water, then stab their prey with their long, dagger-like bills. Fish are startled by movement, so birds feeding together would have less success.

Feeding on fish

Grey herons eat many different types and sizes of fish. The parents regurgitate food for the young but tiny fish are also given to small chicks. Increasingly bigger fish are provided as the chicks grow and nestlings are often given fish that are larger than they can manage.

Fish form most of the heron's diet, but it also eats moles, voles, water shrews and other small mammals caught in the water or on land. Grass snakes are often eaten, as are amphibians – especially frogs. Occasionally, a heron will take a young injured moorhen or a duckling. Herons also feed on freshwater invertebrates, such as shrimps and crayfish. Some vegetation is eaten in order to help form pellets of bones, fur and other indigestible material that remains after prey has been swallowed whole and the rest digested. The pellets are then regurgitated.

Herons eat about 300–500g (10½–17½oz) daily, or about 20–30 per cent of their adult body weight. Anglers used to claim that herons damaged their sport, but commercial fisheries and small rivers are generally well enough stocked to cope with the occasional heron. However, grey heron can kill or wound carp or other fish in a fish pond so garden ponds should be made heron-proof. Ask the RSPB for advice about this.

A heron's broad wings enable it to take off and climb steeply away. This male has collected a twig, which it is taking to its mate to build their nest.

Nesting behaviour

Some heronries may have just a few nests, but several in Britain have 50 and some more than 100. The birds usually return to the same site each year. Most nests are built in the tops of deciduous trees, often more than 20m (66ft) above the ground, and the biggest trees may have half a dozen or more in them. They are fairly conspicuous, particularly while the branches are still bare, but the nests built in coniferous trees are more difficult to see. In plantations, there is usually one per tree, situated close to the trunk. A few nests may be constructed on cliffs or low down among reeds. On some small islands, they may be built on the ground.

Where herons are left undisturbed, they adapt to being near humans. Wild herons nest alongside captive birds at Great Witchingham Wildlife Park in Norfolk, for example, and in London's Regent's Park, grey herons nest on an island in the lake.

GREY HERON FACT FILE

Standing hunched and still, with its flexible neck sunk in an 'S' shape, the grey heron at rest can look relatively unobtrusive. It extends its long neck while fishing and during courtship displays, when it reaches up and then lowers its head over its back, bill pointing skywards.

● **NAMES**
Common names: grey heron, heron
Scientific name: *Ardea cinerea*

● **HABITAT**
Rivers, ponds, lakes and streams with shallow margins; marshes, estuaries and coasts; often hunts on dry land

● **DISTRIBUTION**
Throughout Britain and Ireland

● **STATUS**
Population possibly more than 15,000 in UK; may now be at an all-time high in British Isles

● **SIZE**
Length 90–98cm (36–39in) with extended neck, weight 1–2kg (2–4½lb)

● **KEY FEATURES**
Long legs, long neck, often hunched, and large dagger shaped bill; head, neck and underparts are whitish with long black crest on head and dark stripes on front of neck and breast – the rest of the bird is dove grey; flight feathers are dark, almost black, in flight and legs extend well beyond tail; juveniles have smaller greyer crest, dark crown and darker neck

● **HABITS**
Stands motionless in shallow water, watching for prey; can fly long distances when migrating

● **VOICE**
Typical flight call is a harsh croaking *'fraank'*; squawks, croaks and other calls in the colony.

● **FOOD**
Mainly fish but also amphibians, small mammals, some young and adult birds, insects, crustaceans and reptiles

● **BREEDING**
From early February through to May or even June

● **NEST**
Very large structures made out of twigs; generally located in the tops of high trees; same nest reoccupied each year

● **EGGS**
Usually 4 or 5 large, pale blue eggs; single brood; incubation takes 25–26 days

● **YOUNG**
Fledge at 42–45 days and are looked after for a further 2–3 weeks

The dagger-like bill turns from yellow to pinkish orange early in the breeding season.

When the heron is standing motionless, the wispy, black crest is noticeable.

A large, distinctive black patch on the 'shoulders' reaches along the edge of the flanks and beneath the folded wings.

Underneath its breast feathers, a heron has two patches of 'powder down' which provide a white dust to coagulate fish slime and help in keeping the rest of the bird's plumage clean.

Distribution map key

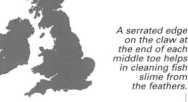

- Present all year round
- Present during summer months
- Present during winter months
- Not present

A serrated edge on the claw at the end of each middle toe helps in cleaning fish slime from the feathers.

A heron has long, wispy whitish plumes on its back, contrasting black and white around the head and a yellow or pinkish orange bill.

Fishing expertise

The grey heron hunts by patrolling the shallows, usually beneath overhanging foliage. It walks slowly against the current and strikes at fish or other aquatic prey.

The heron darts its head forward and spears its prey on its sharp beak. An elongated sixth vertebra in its neck, which can be locked and released, acts like a trigger mechanism and allows the heron to move its head at astounding speed.

The eyes are set in line with the long spear-like bill. They can move within their rigid sockets and swivel forward to give the heron binocular vision. This allows the bird to aim at its prey with great accuracy.

GREY HERON CALENDAR

NOVEMBER • FEBRUARY

Grey herons remain on their territories unless severe cold begins to affect the fish on which they feed. If this happens, the birds will usually move to the coast where the brackish water will still be unfrozen.

MARCH • APRIL

The birds are re-established in their traditional colonies, where nest building and repair continues through the season. Clutches of four or five eggs hatch after almost four weeks' incubation.

MAY • JUNE

Once hatched, the chicks constantly demand to be fed. The parents regurgitate partly digested food into the nest for them, and bring small fish. The chicks leave the nest after six to seven weeks.

JULY

Most of the chicks have fledged and are independent, although they are not yet competent at catching fish. Their parents continue to feed them while they practise.

AUGUST

The young birds disperse in late summer. Some will return early next year to breed in the colonies where they hatched, but others travel to different colonies to breed.

SEPTEMBER • OCTOBER

Most British grey herons do not migrate but this is the peak time for birds from Scandinavia and the Netherlands to arrive to take advantage of the milder winters.

Although prey are generally seized between the two mandibles, a fish is occasionally impaled on the lower part of the bill. In this case, to move the fish from its bill into its mouth, the heron jerks its head backwards. The fish slides from the bill and the heron snatches it in mid-air.

Having positioned the fish so that it lies head first, the heron opens its jaws unusually wide to swallow the fish whole. Several fish can be stored in the crop for transport to the nest.

The grey heron's nest, which is typically about 45cm (18in) across, is made from twigs that the male brings to the female, often having stolen them from other nests. If it is very big, other birds may be attracted to nest in it, too – notably tree sparrows, although these birds are now scarce. The structure is tightly woven so that when the parent birds regurgitate food into the nest for the young to pick up, nothing is lost through leakage.

Migratory patterns

Grey herons from central Europe migrate regularly as far south as west and central east Africa – even Kenya. Ringed birds have also been recovered in the West Indies, Azores, Canary Islands, Madeira, Cape Verde Islands, Iceland and Greenland. However, grey herons in Britain do not always move abroad for winter, but when the weather is very cold they may be forced to travel to the coast if their feeding areas inland freeze up.

Birds arriving to overwinter in Britain from Norway and northern and eastern Europe seem to have no difficulty in accomplishing the lengthy journey across the North Sea – they may have travelled 250–1120km (155–700 miles). When on long migration flights, grey herons do not soar and glide using thermals, as do other large birds, such as storks and many birds of prey. Instead, they mainly use flapping wingbeats, alternating with short glides.

Population increase

For almost 70 years there has been a census of breeding grey herons, which is now run by the British Trust for

Ornithology (BTO). Until recently, the records showed a ceiling of around 4500 pairs, achieved after a succession of mild winters in England and Wales, although the population could be halved in a very cold spell and might take six to eight years to recover.

Shooting was for many years mainly responsible for keeping down grey heron numbers in Britain. However, the bird was afforded full protection more than 20 years ago, and since then numbers have increased. The population has more than doubled since a 1964 census recorded some 6000 breeding pairs.

Herons struggle to find food when lakes and rivers freeze. They head for the coast where the salty water remains unfrozen.

Recognising swifts and swallows

Agile fliers that catch insects on the wing, swifts, swallows and their close relatives, the martins, visit Britain from spring to autumn. Mostly, these birds choose to nest on ledges and in the lofts of old buildings, barns and outhouses.

Parental responsibility for swallows does not end when the young fledge and leave the nest. The brood will stay together for some time, being fed by the parents and often roosting together on the same ledge in a sheltered barn or outhouse.

Visit a lowland lake or wetland in May and there is a good chance of seeing swifts, swallows or martins. If the weather is warm, flying insects – on which the birds feed – will be numerous, creating an opportunity for seeing all four common species. These are the swift, swallow, house martin and sand martin. Alpine swifts and red-rumped swallows appear rarely but annually, especially in southern Britain. Although they can appear at any time during the summer months, most sightings are in spring and autumn.

Swallows and martins are known as hirundines because they belong to the family Hirundinidae. This family is part of a larger grouping called passerines, meaning perching birds. Despite the superficial similarities between swifts and hirundines, they are not related. Swifts are not passerines, and belong to a different family, the Apodidae, meaning 'no legs'. This is something of a misnomer because swifts do have legs, but so short that attempts at walking are ungainly.

Although there are distinct differences between swifts and hirundines, it is easy to see why they are often considered together. They share the same narrow-winged, streamlined appearance suited to spending much time on the wing. Both have extremely small bills but large gapes that help them to feed successfully.

Although they always feed on the wing, swallows and martins also spend some time perching on wires or roofs, and they roost under cover throughout the night. By contrast, swifts land only in order to nest. Otherwise, they feed, drink, sleep, preen, mate and gather nest material in flight. They remain on the wing from the end of one

breeding season to the start of the next or longer. Some young swifts may not land for as much as three or even four years, until they breed for the first time.

Migrating south

Swifts, swallows and martins fly south for the winter, the four common species all wintering in sub-Saharan Africa. Swallows make the longest journey, with large numbers of European birds travelling as far as South Africa.

Sand martins and house martins are often among the first migrant birds to return in spring and small numbers can sometimes be seen in early March, usually concentrated around good feeding areas, such as flooded gravel pits and lakes. Swallows appear soon afterwards, usually around the end of March or beginning of April. All three hirundine species can be badly affected if unseasonably cold weather means that the usual supply of flying insects is not available.

Swifts arrive much later – usually in the first week of May – visiting traditional nest sites and good feeding areas immediately. However, if the weather turns cold on their arrival, it is not unusual for swifts to disappear back south for a few days in search of food.

Building nests

The nesting success of swifts is inextricably linked to the existence of suitable lofts and other man-made structures. These provide shelter from bad weather and protection from predators. Swifts select old buildings, preferring the eaves of larger houses and other edifices, such as church towers. Wherever they breed, swifts make their presence evident with screaming aerial chases between houses and along streets.

Swifts raise a single brood each year, although they sometimes lay replacement clutches if the first eggs are lost due to exceptionally cold weather. Most swifts have left Britain by early August.

Like swifts, swallows often choose man-made sites for their nests. Characteristically, they favour ledges in barns and other types of outhouses and they build their nests using a combination of straw and mud. In a good year, swallows raise two broods.

▲ Mud is the essential building material for the house martin's nest, which is often sited under roof eaves.

◄ Long tail streamers – longer in males than females – help distinguish the swallow from other hirundines and swifts. The pale underparts are also a means of identification.

▲ The house martin's white rump is often most conspicuous as it reaches its nest and hovers near the entrance.

House martins breed in colonies, constructing their mud-cup nests under the eaves of houses and in other urban sites. In Britain, at least, the species has all but abandoned ancestral, natural nest sites such as cliffs. New colonies can be encouraged by placing artificial, half-built nests on the sides of houses. Shortly after their arrival at a nest site, house martins visit nearby puddles to collect pellets of mud to complete the nest. In most years, house martins raise two broods of young, abandoning the colony in August or September.

Soon after their arrival, and immediately the weather shows signs of spring, sand martins congregate in suitable breeding areas. They also nest in colonies and – as their name suggests – prefer sand banks. These make ideal sites because the birds can excavate their nest tunnels easily. Recently, gravel and sand extraction sites, as well as river banks, have been used. In a good year a sand martin pair will have two broods, with the adults and their offspring leaving the nest sites in August.

WILDLIFE WATCH

Where can I see swifts and swallows?

● Swifts, swallows and martins can be found almost anywhere with a good supply of flying insects. Look for swallows and martins between April and September. Swifts can be seen between May and August.

● Swallows feed over open countryside and open water, constantly uttering their 'tswit' twittering calls, or 'tswit tswit' and 'splee-pink' of excitement or alarm. They nest in farm buildings or more urban locations.

● Swifts will often feed over lakes and marshes, especially just after their arrival in May or during cold or rainy weather. Otherwise, look for these birds over known breeding spots in towns and villages; listen for their far-carrying, piercing screams.

● House martins congregate over lakes and flooded gravel pits shortly after their arrival in March and April. Thereafter, they can be found in the vicinity of the nests, under the

eaves of buildings. Watch for birds gathering mud from the margins of puddles and pools. Their calls are drier-sounding than those of swifts and swallows.

● Sand martins may be found nesting in large colonies in sand banks. If the site is close to water, the birds may feed nearby. If it is away from water, they will feed at the nearest lake or marsh. Their calls are the driest, harshest and most rattling of all.

EASY GUIDE TO SPOTTING SWIFTS AND SWALLOWS

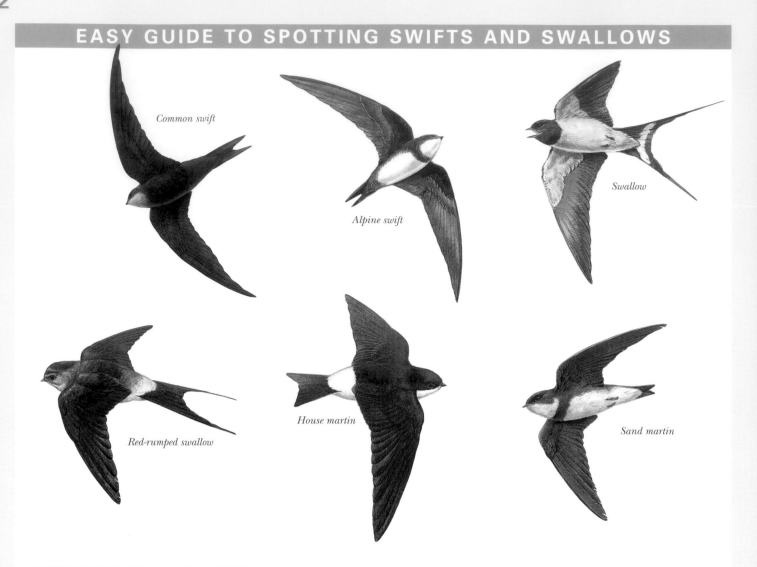

Common swift

Alpine swift

Swallow

Red-rumped swallow

House martin

Sand martin

WHAT ARE SWIFTS AND SWALLOWS?

● Swifts and swallows are characterised by their comparatively long, narrow wings, tiny bills and proportionately large mouths.

● Although swallows and martins are not closely related to swifts, they share the same means of feeding by catching flying insects on the wing in their large gapes.

● Swifts are members of a family of birds called the Apodidae. One species, the common swift, is a frequent summer visitor while a second, the alpine swift, is a rare but annual vagrant.

● Swallows and martins belong to the family Hirundinidae; three species, the swallow, house martin and sand martin, are common summer visitors, while a fourth – the red-rumped swallow – is a rare but annual vagrant.

● Given that swifts, swallows and martins spend much of their time on the wing, it is perhaps not surprising that their legs are tiny compared with those of many other birds. Swallows and martins can walk, to some degree, and they can also perch. Swifts, in contrast, are barely able to shuffle along once on land and are, consequently, very vulnerable to being attacked by predators if they become grounded.

Distribution map key

Present during summer months

Spring and autumn migrant

Not present

HOW CAN I IDENTIFY SWIFTS AND SWALLOWS?

● Swifts are masters of the air and on some days their sickle-shaped wings seldom seem to move. In common with the hirundines, however, when feeding low over water, they often beat their wings rapidly.

● Swallows and martins have variable flight patterns. Depending on the weather conditions, they sometimes adopt purposeful, low-level flight if, for example, hawking for insects low over water; alternatively, they may wheel and glide in seemingly effortless flight on sunny days.

● All these birds feed on flies and small swarming insects such as midges and mosquitoes. They also eat aphids, flying ants and other flying insects. Swifts include airborne spiders in their diet. As well as feeding over water, swifts, swallows and martins often congregate around areas other than water where insects proliferate – for example, farmyards and sewage works. There are no similarly sized birds with which they can be confused.

● Swifts can be recognised in flight by their narrow, swept-back wings and horseshoe-like outline, and their virtually all-dark plumage and pale chin.

● Swallows also have relatively long, narrow wings but their bodies look longer. This impression is emphasised by the long, forked tails of adult birds.

● Swifts, swallows and martins are often easiest to see clearly just before rain falls, especially near a lake. This is because the flying insects on which they feed fly at lower altitudes in this sort of weather.

● Just prior to their autumn migration, swallows and martins often gather in noisy, chattering flocks. The birds frequently perch on overhead wires. These groups usually comprise swallows and house martins but, once in a while, a sand martin may be spotted among them. Swallows and sand martins – but not house martins or swifts – also form big roosts in coastal reedbeds.

● Estimates put the number of swifts breeding in Britain at some 80,000 pairs, with upwards of 20,000 pairs in Ireland.

● About 570,000 pairs of swallows are thought to breed in Britain, and there are an estimated 250,000 pairs in Ireland.

COMMON SWIFT *Apus apus*

With its long, narrow wings held swept-back in a sickle-like outline and its all-dark plumage, the common swift is easily recognisable. Even when in rapid, low-level flight, it holds its wings unfolded and stiff. The bird looks short-headed and long-tailed in flight, with the forked tail often held closed. Although adult plumage is very dark brown, it usually appears black, especially when seen against the light. A good sighting reveals its pale throat. The juvenile is similar to the adult, but with a shorter tail and pale margins to the feathers on its upperparts.

While feeding their hungry young, swifts need to make frequent visits to their nests in the roofs of houses or other buldings.

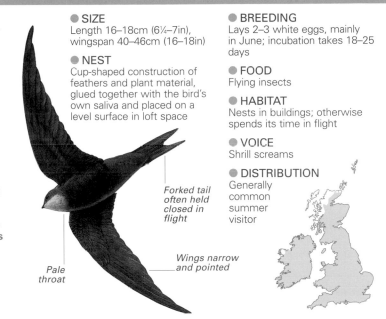

Pale throat

Forked tail often held closed in flight

Wings narrow and pointed

- **SIZE**
Length 16–18cm (6¼–7in), wingspan 40–46cm (16–18in)
- **NEST**
Cup-shaped construction of feathers and plant material, glued together with the bird's own saliva and placed on a level surface in loft space
- **BREEDING**
Lays 2–3 white eggs, mainly in June; incubation takes 18–25 days
- **FOOD**
Flying insects
- **HABITAT**
Nests in buildings; otherwise spends its time in flight
- **VOICE**
Shrill screams
- **DISTRIBUTION**
Generally common summer visitor

ALPINE SWIFT *Apus melba*

Similar in outline to the common swift, the alpine swift is larger with a white throat and underparts, and a brown breast band. The alpine swift's wingbeats are often slower than those of the common swift but with a deeper action. Rare though annual visitors to Britain, alpine swifts often mix with feeding flocks of common swifts, when differences in size, markings and behaviour become apparent.

The alpine swift's largely white underparts are distinctive but its white throat is often difficult to see when the bird is in flight.

White throat and belly separated by dark collar

Conspicuous white underparts

Wings long, narrow and pointed at tip

- **SIZE**
Length 20–23cm (8–9in), wingspan 52–58cm (20½–23in)
- **NEST**
Does not nest in Britain
- **BREEDING**
Does not breed in Britain
- **FOOD**
Flying insects
- **HABITAT**
Skies often over marshes and lakes
- **VOICE**
Generally silent
- **DISTRIBUTION**
Rare wanderer to Britain and Ireland; most recorded sightings in spring when birds overshoot their normal southern European breeding range

SWALLOW *Hirundo rustica*

Often perching in pairs on wires in spring, swallows also congregate where flying insects are abundant, and gather in large flocks in autumn. Their upperparts are dark blue with blackish flight feathers. The tail feathers are black with white patches near the ends, and outer feathers form streamers that are longer in the male. A red forehead and throat contrast with white to pale buff underparts. Juveniles have duller face colouring and shorter tail forks.

Swallows are agile fliers, able to negotiate sudden twists and turns. This is useful for catching fast-moving insects, and finding their way into barns and other outbuildings.

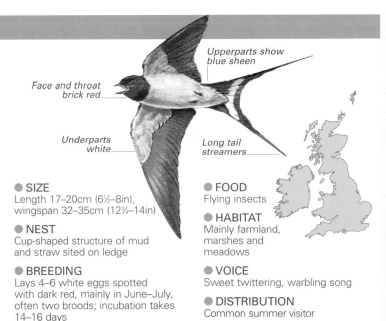

Face and throat brick red

Underparts white

Upperparts show blue sheen

Long tail streamers

- **SIZE**
Length 17–20cm (6½–8in), wingspan 32–35cm (12¾–14in)
- **NEST**
Cup-shaped structure of mud and straw sited on ledge
- **BREEDING**
Lays 4–6 white eggs spotted with dark red, mainly in June–July, often two broods; incubation takes 14–16 days
- **FOOD**
Flying insects
- **HABITAT**
Mainly farmland, marshes and meadows
- **VOICE**
Sweet twittering, warbling song
- **DISTRIBUTION**
Common summer visitor

RED-RUMPED SWALLOW *Hirundo daurica*

The flight of the red-rumped swallow tends to be more leisurely than that of the swallow. Adults have dark blue upperwings, back and crown with pale, faintly streaked underparts. The tail is dark with long, incurved streamers. Juveniles are similar but with shorter and paler tail streamers. The red-rumped swallow's behaviour is similar to that of the swallow with which it sometimes mixes. Rather surprisingly, this species is sometimes recorded well after swallows have left in autumn and in advance of their return in early spring.

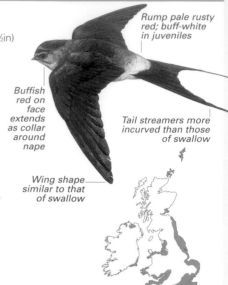

Rump pale rusty red; buff-white in juveniles

Buffish red on face extends as collar around nape

Tail streamers more incurved than those of swallow

Wing shape similar to that of swallow

- **SIZE**
  Length 14–19cm (5½–7½in), wingspan 32–34cm (12¾–13½in)
- **NEST**
  Does not nest in Britain
- **BREEDING**
  Does not breed in Britain
- **FOOD**
  Flying insects
- **HABITAT**
  Coasts and wetlands
- **VOICE**
  Generally silent but has distinctive long, nasal '*rtseek*'
- **DISTRIBUTION**
  Rare but regular visitor, coinciding with either spring or autumn migration

A red-rumped swallow lands at the edge of a pool, perhaps to collect mud for its nest. In common with other swallows and martins, its legs are strong enough to launch it back into the air.

HOUSE MARTIN *Delichon urbica*

This familiar, recognisable summer visitor usually nests under the eaves of houses and sometimes in loose colonies. Then the birds can be seen sitting on nearby wires or circling overhead. Adults have mainly dark blue upperparts contrasting with a pure white rump and white underparts. The tail is slightly forked but can look square-ended. Juveniles are similar with not such white underparts.

Upperparts dark with blue sheen

Wings triangular in outline

White rump

- **SIZE**
  Length 12.5–14cm (4¾–5½in), wingspan 26–29cm (10½–11½in)
- **NEST**
  Cup-shaped mud nest built under house eaves
- **BREEDING**
  Lays 3–5 white eggs, mainly in May–June; incubation takes 14–16 days
- **FOOD**
  Flying insects
- **HABITAT**
  Nests on buildings; often feeds over water
- **VOICE**
  Simple, brief chirping song
- **DISTRIBUTION**
  Generally common summer visitor

House martins repair their nests throughout the breeding season by adding mud.

SAND MARTIN *Riparia riparia*

A well-known summer visitor, it is easy to recognise the adult sand martin by its uniformly sandy brown upperparts and rather triangular-shaped wings. Its underparts are white except for a dark chest band, underwings and tail. The juvenile is similar except that the feathers on its upperparts have pale margins, giving a scaly appearance.

Upperparts sandy brown

Underparts pale except for a distinctive dark collar

- **SIZE**
  Length 12–13cm (4¾–5in), wingspan 26–29cm (10½–11½in)
- **NEST**
  In tunnel excavated in sand bank; nests in colonies
- **BREEDING**
  Lays 4–6 white eggs, mainly in May–June, often attempting a second brood; incubation takes about 14 days
- **FOOD**
  Flying insects
- **HABITAT**
  Rivers with sandy banks, gravel pits; often feeds over water
- **VOICE**
  Quiet, hard twittering song and harsh grating call
- **DISTRIBUTION**
  Common summer visitor

Sand martins usually make a direct approach to their nest burrows, pausing briefly at the entrance before they disappear from view.

The osprey

When an osprey plunges from the sky and, amid a shower of spray, plucks a fish from just under the water's surface, its prey seldom escapes from the lethal grip of razor-sharp talons.

Occurring on every continent except Antarctica, the spectacular osprey is one of the world's most successful and numerous birds of prey. In Britain, until very recently, it bred only in Scotland, but now a few pairs breed in England, and ospreys may appear on inland waters almost anywhere in the country during the spring and autumn migration.

Essentially a land bird, the osprey has adapted to catching fish, using an extraordinary technique that involves plunging into the water, seizing its heavy prey and hauling it up into the air in an exhibition of gravity-defying power. It is equipped with very strong, sharp-clawed feet that enable it to grab and hold on to its slippery, struggling quarry, dense water-repellent plumage to prevent it becoming waterlogged and unable to fly, and a hooked bill for tearing its prey to pieces.

The osprey specialises in an apparently reckless diving technique to seize its slippery meal, unlike most other birds of prey that hunt fish, which try to avoid immersion in the water.

Sudden dive

A hunting osprey generally flies over the water at a height of 10–40m (33–130ft), staring intently downwards for any sign of a vulnerable fish. It will try to catch fish that are swimming very close to the surface, and never attempts to catch anything swimming much deeper than a metre (3ft) or so. The bird is able to target its prey through rippling water even when the surface is dappled by falling rain, and it is only defeated by very windy weather that whips up the surface into small waves.

Once an osprey has targeted a fish, it generally hovers in the wind to pinpoint its exact position before hurtling down in

PALE DISGUISE

The strikingly contrasted brown and white plumage of the osprey suits the bird's hunting technique. Fish are always alert to danger. They are especially aware of what is happening in the air above them, because this is where many of their predators come from, so any fish-hunter needs to be as inconspicuous as possible. The brightness of the sky means that white plumage usually provides the best camouflage, blending with the background. Accordingly, the osprey has pale feathers on its underparts. There is a patch of white on its head too, since this area is also visible to fish when the bird swoops over a lake. Ideally, the osprey would also have all-white wings and a white tail, but pale feathers are much weaker than dark ones and the bird's flight feathers need to be as strong as possible to enable it to take off from the water with its prey.

Diving attack

Ospreys are skilled aerial hunters that have perfected the art of plunge-diving after fish. Each bird hones its own technique by practice and experience, but a typical osprey strike usually follows the same pattern of patrol, hover, plunge and recovery.

Once it spots a potential meal, the bird trails its long legs in a relaxed fashion to help reduce speed during a gliding descent.

When out hunting, the osprey alternately beats its wings and glides as it cruises above the water, looking for a fish swimming close to the surface.

Close to stalling, the osprey dips its tail momentarily to keep control as it hovers briefly over its target…

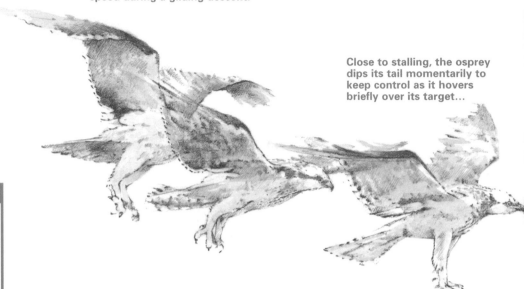

MIGRATION

The Scottish osprey population is the most westerly group of breeding ospreys in Europe. Since starting to recolonise Scotland 50 years ago they have established a successful breeding population. These birds migrate via south-west Europe to winter in West Africa. The return journey does not begin until March or early April, as there is little point in the birds arriving back to breed when the water in some Scottish lochs may be frozen.

The birds passing through Britain on migration are mostly Scottish breeders, but Swedish and Norwegian ringed birds have been recorded breeding in Scotland. A few Scandinavian breeders may deliberately migrate through the extreme south and east of England. Others are vagrants, blown off-course by strong winds.

Very keen eyesight allows the osprey to locate prey beneath the surface of the water in most weather conditions. The bird can even judge the depth at which fish are swimming.

its trademark plunging dive. Just before the bird hits the water it throws its talons forwards and folds its wings backwards and upwards. This minimises resistance as the osprey slices into the water. Once it has a grip on its victim it beats its wings powerfully downwards to pull itself and its prize free of the water's grip and back up into the air. The osprey's strong feet are equipped with an intricate pattern of tiny sharp spikes, called spicules, that provide an excellent grip on its slippery, struggling prey as it flies off. Big fish are taken to the nearest dry land or tree to be eaten, although the bird may have to wait for several minutes for its victim to die.

Although most of the fish targeted by ospreys weigh less than a kilogram (2lb), they may sometimes take much larger salmon, carp, pike or perch. These can easily weigh twice as much as the bird itself, and it takes an enormous effort for the osprey to pull itself free of the water with such an enormous, unwieldy burden. Occasionally the bird may overreach itself and strike at a such large prey that it cannot lift it, and is forced to let it go. However, the very best hunters have been known to catch two fish in a single dive, seizing one in each foot.

Washing and preening

The osprey often washes its feet by trailing them in the water as it flies low over the surface, and after each kill it spends time cleaning scraps of fish from its talons and beak. It preens and oils its plumage regularly, using oil taken from

the well-developed preen gland at the base of the tail. This helps prevent waterlogging when the bird plunges into the water after its prey. Ospreys have also mastered the art of shaking themselves in mid-flight to rid themselves of excess water. Much of this behaviour is instinctive, but the hunting skills take time to perfect. It may take young ospreys several months to learn to fish efficiently.

Transient visitors

As they migrate to and from their winter quarters in Africa and along the Mediterranean, ospreys seem to be drawn to water shining in the distance, and frequently stop off for a few days to rest and feed. In Britain, many inland waters have plentiful fish populations, offering more than enough prey to satisfy an osprey, and the arrival of such a spectacular bird is likely to be welcomed, unlike some other fish-eating birds. Cormorants, for example, often flock in large numbers, and such flocks can catch huge quantities of fish with their effective hunting technique – the birds simply dive down from the surface to catch unwary fish swimming too close to the surface. Ospreys, however, are more often found hunting alone, and during the short time that they stay, they do not have a detrimental effect on fish stocks.

In Scotland, most fishery owners do not begrudge ospreys the prey that they take, despite the high value of many of the fish,

COURTSHIP AND NESTING

Ospreys do not usually breed until their third, fourth or even fifth year, but two-year-olds often pair up during the breeding season and build practice nests. This is no bad thing, as the construction of a nest from scratch is a big undertaking. It can take even experienced pairs as long as two or three weeks, even when a good structure remains from the year before. Osprey nests, which are usually sited near the top of conifer trees, need to be very big and sturdy to support two or three fast-growing chicks, plus their parents, for almost two months.

The male bird is responsible for the main frame of the nest, bringing back long twigs and substantial branches and completing most of the

Ospreys such as these mating birds form monogamous pairs, because it takes both parents to raise a brood of chicks. There is no opportunity for the male to father a second brood with another female. However, it is not certain whether these bonds endure from year to year.

construction work. When the nest itself has been finished, the female adds the finishing touches, lining the nest with moss, bark, small twigs and grass. The birds return every year, renovating the old nest and adding more material so it grows bigger and bigger. Eventually the nest can become so huge that the tree may collapse beneath its weight, and the birds have to begin again on a new site.

Ospreys make attentive parents, stripping morsels of fish from the prey that they bring back to the nest and then delicately presenting them to their young.

which may include salmon and trout. It is even said that the ornamental fish ponds in front of one Scottish stately home were deliberately stocked with trout to attract ospreys, and provide the spectacle of the birds plunging into the water for the laird's entertainment.

Ospreys are not attracted to freshwater rivers, lakes and ponds exclusively. They often hunt for fish in brackish water or even in the sea. The sizeable fish that ospreys prefer rarely swim close to the surface in the sea, but in very shallow coastal waters small flatfish make easy prey for these skilled hunters. One Scottish study has reported that ospreys often take small

flounders, and that at least two thirds of their attempts to catch them are successful – a high score for a predator.

None of the Scottish breeding birds rely entirely on saltwater fishing for their prey, but around the Mediterranean – where many ospreys are year-round residents – and in many other parts of the species' vast range, ospreys have virtually no freshwater hunting sites and feed exclusively upon sea fish.

With less than a wingspan of height remaining, the osprey makes two powerful hover beats of its large wings. If it has judged the attack well, it is able to pluck its prey from just below the surface and keep flying.

...and then plunges down, swinging its legs forwards with outspread talons and thrusting them out in front of its head.

If it has targeted a large or deeply swimming fish, the osprey may crash right into the water and become submerged. It extricates itself as quickly as possible to avoid becoming waterlogged.

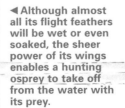

◄ Although almost all its flight feathers will be wet or even soaked, the sheer power of its wings enables a hunting osprey to take off from the water with its prey.

OSPREY FACT FILE

A specialist fish hunter, the osprey has waterproof plumage and nostrils that can be closed as it plunges into the water, which it often does with a great splash. Legs with no feathers make it easy for the bird to clean off fish scales.

Seen at close range, the osprey has a conspicuously hooked bill, a dark mask and staring yellow eyes.

● NAMES
Common name: osprey
Scientific name: *Pandion haliaetus*

● HABITAT
Lakes, rivers and coastal waters

● DISTRIBUTION
Scottish Highlands and a few places in England; reintroduced from 1996 at Rutland Water, Leicestershire and has started to recolonise the Lake District; migrants occur sporadically elsewhere

● STATUS
Generally rare, but 160 pairs now breed in Scotland plus a few pairs in England

● SIZE
Length 52–60cm (20–24in); weight 1.2–2kg (2½–4½lb)

● KEY FEATURES
Larger than buzzard, with much longer wings and proportionately shorter tail; underparts and inner wing gleaming white, with dark 'wrist' patch at angle of wing; brown tail and wing coverts; white head with speckled crown and dark stripe through eye; female larger than male

● HABITS
Hunts for fish from the air; usually hovers briefly before diving down to catch prey just under the water's surface

● VOICE
Rather silent away from nesting site and in absence of dependent young; otherwise a varied vocabulary of high-pitched whistles, barks and squeals

● FOOD
Fish, averaging about 300g (10½oz) each; often brings 6 or 8 fish to nest in one day to feed brood; many Scottish birds feed on trout during breeding season

● BREEDING
Eggs laid April–September, one clutch

● NEST
Huge structures, dominating pine trees in which they are built; added to each year; diameter can exceed 1.5m (5ft), with height of 2m (6½ft); will use artificial nesting platforms

● EGGS
Lays 2–4 white or cream eggs with reddish, brown or lilac blotches and streaks; incubation starts when first egg laid; eggs hatch at 5–6 weeks at 48-hour intervals

● YOUNG
Assiduously tended by parents for first week, but both parents may be absent most of the time at 3 or 4 weeks; fledge at 45–60 days but looked after by parents for further 2 months – sometimes adults and young migrate together

Distribution map key

Present in summer only

Facial markings are brown and white.

Upperparts are uniformly dark brown.

As well as long, curved, sharp talons, the large feet have tiny spikes on the underside for gripping prey.

The medium length tail is barred beneath, the terminal bar being the broadest.

Easy targets

The osprey was quite common in Britain until the 17th century, with up to 1000 breeding pairs recorded – many in England. During the late 18th and 19th centuries, however, it was persecuted by gamekeepers, fish bailiffs and others, and its eggs and skins were in demand for museums and gentlemen's collections. Being large and conspicuous, ospreys made easy targets, and by the middle of the 19th century the breeding population of England had been wiped out.

Ospreys continued to breed in Scotland for another 60 years, but relentless persecution took its toll and the last recorded breeding attempt in Britain during this period took place on Loch Loyne in 1916. That seemed to be the end of the osprey's history as a British breeding bird. Some were occasionally seen in the spring as they migrated across Britain to their breeding areas in Scandinavia, but none remained on British soil for long. It is possible that single birds may have stayed in Britain for the summer in the 1930s, but it was not thought at all likely that two ospreys would encounter each other, pair up and stay to breed. However, this is exactly what did happen at Loch Garten in 1954, and despite setbacks the birds have continued to thrive there. About 160 breeding pairs populate the area now, and ospreys are also breeding in the English Lake District. They have even been successfully introduced to lowland England at Rutland Water, in Leicestershire, where they have bred since 2001.

However, even this success story has been beset by problems. Despite guards, egg collectors succeeded in robbing the Loch Garten nest on several occasions, and other nests have also been plundered. Adult ospreys have died flying into wires, have become lost during migration, or had their nests blown out of trees. There have also been cases where an adult male has deserted its mate and nest in favour of another female. These triumphs and setbacks have been followed with great interest by experts and amateurs alike, and more people have seen the original nest at Loch Garten than any other wild bird's nest in Britain. The revival of the osprey as a breeding species is one of the great wildlife success stories of the current era.

OSPREY CALENDAR

DECEMBER ● FEBRUARY

The ospreys that breed in Britain spend the winter in West Africa, although some may move to Mediterranean regions as the spring migration approaches. There they prepare for journey to Scotland – a series of short flights with stops to rest and feed.

MARCH ● MAY

Adult birds complete the journey more swiftly than younger ones. Two or three-year-old birds that will not breed may linger in non-breeding areas before reaching their destination. Eggs are laid from April and both parents look after the chicks.

JUNE ● AUGUST

The young birds are educated in fishing techniques by their parents. Adult birds continue to look after their young for about eight weeks after they leave the nest.

SEPTEMBER ● NOVEMBER

The birds begin their migration southwards, often resting on rivers, lakes or reservoirs on the way. They tend to return to the same waters every year.

The osprey is afforded full protection at all times under Schedule 1 of the Wildlife and Countryside Act 1981. Interference with the bird or its nest, eggs or young is prohibited with strict penalties for anyone infringing the law.

WILDLIFE WATCH

Where can I see ospreys?

● The best way to see ospreys is at nesting sites in Scotland, where there are visitor centres and proper viewing hides – even closed circuit television. Some, such as the RSPB site at Loch Garten, are prime breeding sites for the species year after year, but others, while popular at first, may suddenly be deserted by the birds. Ospreys are also now breeding at Rutland Water in Leicestershire and in Cumbria. Local Tourist Information Centres will have details of the current situation.

● Seeing the birds fishing, and possibly eating prey nearby, can be much more interesting than watching a nest site. The hunting territory may be several miles away from the nest site.

● At RSPB sites wardens can advise when the male may be returning to the nest with a fish for the female or chicks.

● More than 100 osprey nesting sites around Scotland have no viewing facilities. Watching at these may disturb the birds, which is a criminal offence. Large nests can be very obvious and a bird leaving the nest is an immediate signal to leave the area.

● Migrant ospreys often appear at reservoirs or lakes throughout Britain in spring and autumn. If they can find food easily, they may stay for several days, so it is well worth visiting a site where an osprey has been recently seen.

While incubating eggs, ospreys are generally unobtrusive and difficult to spot. Often the only indication of the presence of a sitting bird is when a head peers briefly over the rim of the nest. The bird itself is dwarfed by the massive structure of its nest.

The pike

Thanks to its acute senses for detecting prey, as well as a mouthful of sharp teeth, this freshwater fish is a fearsome predator. The pike feeds on other fish, waterfowl, amphibians and even its own kind.

Known as an ambush predator, the pike has a long, narrow body that can slide easily between the stems of water plants and reeds. It is camouflaged against its surroundings by the greenish yellow stripes covering its body. Large eyes towards the front of the head allow binocular vision and accurate judgement of distance – crucial when stalking prey. Its dorsal and anal fins are set well back towards the tail, allowing the pike to achieve sudden and powerful acceleration when it flexes its body. A stalking pike edges towards its intended prey with imperceptible movements of its transparent pectoral (chest) fins. Once within lunging distance, the pike contracts its body into an 'S' shape. Springing straight again in a sudden movement throws the pike forwards. It opens its mouth wide, sucking both water and the unsuspecting prey deep inside.

Once the pike closes its mouth, the creature is impaled on the large, sickle-shaped teeth of its upper and lower jaws. Numerous backward-pointing smaller teeth on both the roof of its mouth and tongue hold the prey firmly in place. The only chance it has to escape is during the 'turning period' when the pike juggles it into a head-first swallowing position. If the prey has a set of sharp spines, such as those of sticklebacks, perch or ruffe, the pike may spit it out.

Special senses
The pike does not hunt by sight alone. Along its lower jaw and on either side of its head, rows of sensory pits detect the tiny electrical currents emitted by all living animals. Fish cannot move without generating these small electrical fields and also vibrations, which carry through the water to the waiting pike. Lateral lines that run down each side of the pike's body pick up vibrations from the surrounding water. Nostrils on the pike's snout contain large, highly sensitive nasal membranes that allow the fish to detect small amounts of dissolved chemicals in the water, so the pike has an excellent sense of smell.

In murky, turgid waters, and in clear waters at night, these mechanisms for detecting prey become more important for the pike than sight. There are many accounts of blind pike maintaining body condition. This is most likely because they were able to catch enough food by using their other senses.

Prehistoric predator
Pike have an ancient pedigree. Fossil beds in Norfolk's Cromer Forest have yielded superbly detailed pike fossils half a million years old, which look exactly like pike today. In Canada, 60 million-year-old pike fossils have been recovered. It seems that the pike was always perfectly formed for survival so, over many thousands of generations, there has been no need for it to change or adapt.

The pike, ever alert, lurks in the murky depths. It has a good sense of smell as well as excellent eyesight, and can detect the movement of potential prey in the water.

Forward-facing eyes allow the pike to judge how far away its quarry is, and the direction it is travelling from, so it can launch a precise attack.

PIKE FACT FILE

A long fish with a narrow, blade-like body shape, the pike's fins are located well back towards the tail, allowing powerful acceleration when the fish needs to surge forward to attack its prey, but not permitting sustained fast swimming. The pike is an ambush specialist and will not chase prey over any distance.

● **NAME**
Common name: pike
Scientific name: *Esox lucius*

● **HABITAT**
Reedy backwaters

● **DISTRIBUTION**
Freshwater throughout
British Isles

● **STATUS**
Generally healthy but numbers unknown; no evidence of declines in bodies of water that have been monitored, such as Lake Windermere

● **SIZE**
Length up to 1.5m (5ft); average weight of male 4–5kg (8¾–11lb), female around 14kg (31lb); occasional monster specimens may weigh 20kg (44lb) or more

● **KEY FEATURES**
Long narrow body with yellow and green stripes; wide mouth with sharp teeth, smaller teeth on roof of mouth and tongue; unmistakable among British freshwater fish

● **HABITS**
Stays among weeds, close to banks of ponds, lakes and slow-moving streams and rivers

● **FOOD**
Young eat aquatic invertebrates, fish fry, then larger fish; adults also take frogs, toads, water voles, rats, ducklings and other waterfowl, often cannibalistic

● **BREEDING**
Spawns in late winter or spring, close to water's edge; females lay 9000–20,000 eggs per kg (2lb) of body weight

● **YOUNG**
Pale green at first but soon darken and develop adult colouring

The pattern of vertical stripes along a pike's body provides perfect camouflage among reed stems and water weeds.

Distribution map key

■ Present all year round

□ Not present

Frantically paddling feet of young ducklings are easily detected by the vibration-sensitive lateral line down the side of the pike's body.

Not only is the long, narrow snout streamlined, but it can open extremely wide, allowing the fish to swallow very large prey.

Pectoral fins are used for slow, stealthy swimming among the weeds.

Pelvic fins, set well back along the body, are used for steering and braking.

The anal fin, together with the dorsal fin above and the tail, is used to propel the pike forward.

However, during the course of evolution, many hunted species have changed to fend off various predators, including the pike. A good example of this 'evolutionary arms-race' is the gradual development of hard, sharp spines from soft fin rays, which are offputting to predators such as the pike. A more subtle adaptation is the 'alarm substance' that minnows release from damaged skin cells when they are injured by a predator. This chemical alerts the shoal to danger.

Eggs and hatching

Male pike usually mature at two or three years old and females around a year later. The females spawn in late winter or spring in warm weather when water temperatures reach 6–7°C (42–44°F). Depending on which part of the countryside they are in, pike spawn at different times between February and May. They lay their small, sticky reddish or brownish eggs in batches. These stick to twigs and vegetation, rather than falling into the soft, suffocating silt below. Pike are very productive – females lay 9000–20,000 eggs per kilogram (2lb) of body weight, and a big fish therefore deposits hundreds of thousands of eggs. Not many of the hatchlings need survive to maintain the population.

The hatchlings have a special sticky pad on the back of their heads that attaches to a plant stem. Here they hang motionless while they absorb their yolk sacs and develop their fins in preparation for a free-swimming predatory life.

Voracious appetite

Young pike, called 'jacks', eat aquatic invertebrates, then fish fry, graduating to larger fish as they grow. They normally select fish prey 10–15 per cent of their own weight, but can swallow prey of up to 40 per cent of their body weight. This means that a 10kg (22lb) pike – by no

The pectoral and pelvic fins of a large pike appear disproportionately small. They are used mainly to keep the fish steady in the water and for slow, quiet movement.

means an unusual specimen – can eat a 4kg (8¾lb) trout or salmon. A pike weighing 6.3kg (13¾lb) has been known to swallow another pike weighing 3.2kg (7lb). Researchers have estimated that a pike weighing about 2kg (4½lb) typically needs to eat 21kg (46lb) of food per year to maintain its body weight. In order to grow by 1kg (2lb), however, a pike usually needs to eat about 5–6kg (11–13lb). In an Irish lough, a population of a little more than 1000 pike was estimated to eat over 50–55 tonnes of trout in a single year.

Flexible about what they eat, pike also feed on frogs, water voles, rats, ducklings and even fully grown waterfowl. There are accounts of pike attempting to swallow the heads of swans as the birds feed on underwater weeds. Pike have even been known to seize the hand of a person trailing it over the side of a boat, and to attack a dog wading in shallow water. They will usually try to eat any animal – alive or dead – that is not too big for them to swallow. Pike have even choked to death while trying to swallow other pike of around their own size. Their ability to swallow a large body mass is impressive. If the prey, such as a trout or

Cannibalistic tendencies

From a young age, pike eat fry of their own species. Quarry fish are not much smaller than the predator and such enormous meals mean that the young pike grows fast, making it more likely to dominate the local food supply.

Once a jack has grown to a few centimetres in length, it will be confident enough to approach slightly smaller fry.

As long as the jack can grip the fry head first with its backward-pointing teeth, there is little chance of escape.

This means that the young pike is committed to swallowing its prey, and may choke if it has been over-ambitious.

Such a large meal will take a long time to digest, and may sustain the pike for weeks. Pike caught by anglers often have empty stomachs, suggesting that meals are few and far between.

moorhen, is too long to be swallowed in one gulp, the pike leaves the tail sticking out of its mouth while the front end is being digested in its stomach.

Pike are cannibals, with some populations able to survive where there are few other fish. The youngsters eat invertebrates, such as shrimps, mayfly nymphs and damselfly larvae, then switch to their siblings. Even where other prey is plentiful, pike are cannibalistic from a young age. When the fastest growing individuals reach a sufficient size, they turn on their siblings and swallow them. This can happen when the larger fry are only 3–5cm (1¼–2in) long. Once they have achieved this advantage, the young pike grow even faster, feeding on large numbers of their smaller relatives.

This propensity for cannibalism means that pike populations may be self-regulating – when numbers are high cannibalism is rife, and vice versa. Perch are also known for this behaviour, and it may be a more widespread phenomenon among fish than is generally realised.

Introducing new predators

There is currently a great deal of interest in stocking British waters with other predatory fish – the two most popular options are the zander (pike-perch) and the wels catfish. To do this legally, consents are required from the Environment Agency and English Nature because both of these fish have the potential to spread new parasites and diseases among existing British fish stocks. Naturalists are also concerned about how various prey species might decline in number with the introduction of new predators, and how competition for food might affect the pike.

If a lot of large continental catfish are introduced, then the northern pike might no longer be the largest predatory fish in British waters. Wels catfish can live a long time and reach several hundred pounds in weight. They commonly eat fully grown waterfowl and the largest prey fish, so the concern about their potential impact on freshwater wildlife is understandable.

BIG PIKE

While female pike may live for more than 20 years and grow to prodigious sizes, males seldom grow heavier than about 5kg (11lb). As pike are cannibals, this means that males are at risk of being consumed by the larger females.

There is often speculation as to just how big pike grow in British waters – the answer is remarkably large. For example, in the early 1930s on the marshes at the mouth of the River Endrick where it empties into Loch Lomond, the carcass of a mighty pike was discovered. The fish had been stranded by receding floodwaters. If this occured in springtime, then the pike was certainly a female heading for, or returning from, the spawning grounds. Impressed by its size, the pike's discoverer cut off the head – which measured 32cm (12¾in) after drying – for preservation. Then, 30 or so years on, the late Richard Walker, a famous angler and naturalist, estimated a weight of around 34kg (75lb) for this pike, which would mean that it was about 1.5m (5ft) long. It seems likely that the larger Scottish and Irish lakes, such as Lochs Lomond and Ken and Loughs Corrib, Mask and Erne, may still possibly have the potential to provide enough food for pike to grow to these proportions. The plentiful prey in these lakes includes resident trout and charr, and migratory salmon and sea trout.

Spawning in spring

Pike normally live a solitary life, but in early spring, pregnant, or 'gravid', females ready to spawn may attract the attention of two or three smaller males, which will pursue her, vying for the chance to fertilise her eggs. Neither parent plays a role in looking after the young – quite the opposite in fact. A baby pike might easily be snapped up by one of its parents if it does not stay in the safety of shallow water.

The baby fish develops inside an egg, nourished by the large yolk. Many eggs will be washed away or eaten before the free-swimming fry emerge.

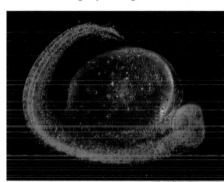

Females release their eggs close to the bank, where they settle among weeds. These will both shelter the baby fish and provide them with a rich supply of invertebrate food.

The stickleback

This aggressive little fish spends most of its life choosing and defending territory among the weed beds of slow-moving streams. At spawning time, the male builds nests and cares for the young.

A close examination of any still or slow-flowing water in spring is likely to be rewarded by the sight of small fish in the shallows, darting around and apparently guarding small areas of the pond or stream bed. These fish are sticklebacks, so named because of the row of sharp spines, or 'stickles', that have developed from the dorsal fins on their backs. These spines can be raised and locked in place during courtship and threat displays.

In Britain, there are two species of freshwater stickleback – the three-spined and the nine-spined. Bold and pugnacious, the males will fight to protect the breeding spots that they have chosen. In suitable habitats a large number of them compete for the best places, and consequently they are well spread out,

each one occupying an area of perhaps half a square metre (5sq ft). Each male builds a nest at the centre of his territory, to receive the eggs of mature females. Sticklebacks are unusual in this, for very few of the world's fish build nests.

Courting colours

At spawning time a male three-spined stickleback develops brilliant blue eyes and a bright red throat that extends over the front of the flanks and belly. These glowing colours help him court one or more egg-filled females. He leads a female to his nest by performing a zigzag dance. The nest, located on the stream bed, is a flat, camouflaged structure comprising fragments of weed glued together with sticky threads made of special secretions from the fish's kidneys.

The nine-spined stickleback is slimmer than the three-spined. In freshwater, they live for no more than three years, spawning once.

The much smaller nine-spined stickleback male develops a far more subdued breeding coloration in spring – generally dark with a jet-black throat patch, although the eyes and pelvic fins become bluish. The courtship dance comprises a series of subtle head-down bobbing jumps. These serve to entice the female to the nest, usually built inside a sheltered weed bed, either on the bottom or suspended from the weeds.

Once at the nest, the male stickleback of either species points to the entrance with the tip of his snout, to encourage the female to burrow in and release her eggs. The male then fertilises them and, in the case of some three-spined sticklebacks, may try to court other females. If successful, a male may amass several clutches, each of 50–100 or more eggs, over the course of a few hectic hours.

Lone parent

Unusually, the male stickleback provides all the parental care. Among the few other species that do this are bullheads and sea horses. As soon as the eggs are laid the female disappears, leaving the male to protect and maintain the nest. The male fans the eggs with his fins, driving a current of freshwater through them until they hatch. This may take from one to three weeks, depending on the temperature of the water.

During this time the male expends much energy on irrigating his eggs and has few opportunities to feed. He is also conspicuous to predators, such as herons, kingfishers and pike. Perhaps because of this risk, stickleback males tending eggs have a muted coloration, reducing the risk of being seen. The problems of parental care do not stop there, however.

ADAPTABLE FISH

The three-spined stickleback is a very common fish. It occurs in many habitats, ranging from peaty upland lochs and burns to richer lowland clay valley rivers and chalk streams, canals, small ponds, lakes, estuaries and even coastal sea water. It varies in size from diminutive Hebridean freshwater forms that have no spines, and mature at around 3cm (1¼in) long, to strapping specimens that are armoured with long sharp spines and grow to about 10cm (4in) long. This variety of habitat, growth and external appearance, together with its elaborate courtship, male parental care and small numbers of large eggs, make it an unusual species. It seems that this small fish is evolving to colonise as many different types of aquatic habitat as possible.

▶ A three-spined stickleback leads a female towards his nest.

◀ Sticky kidney secretions help the three-spined stickleback to glue his nest together.

The male has to defend the eggs from hungry flatworms, snails and other fish, including females of his own species. Even after the eggs have hatched, the young fry need looking after, usually for about five to eight days, until they disperse to fend for themselves. Most males die soon afterwards, emaciated and exhausted.

Few sticklebacks survive to adulthood – which may be why male marine sticklebacks, unlike their freshwater cousins, go through more than one breeding cycle each year, and females can lay several successive batches of eggs.

▲ Found in rock pools around the coast, the 15-spined marine stickleback is quite different from the freshwater species, with a slim, cylindrical body. Up to 15cm (6in) long, this fish does not make nests.

▶ A nine-spined stickleback male in subdued breeding colours guards his territory while looking for a mate.

WILDLIFE WATCH

Where can I watch sticklebacks?

● Look into any still or slow-moving water, while lying quietly on the bank. Polaroid sunglasses can help cut down surface glare.

● Three-spined sticklebacks are easily caught with a net and will live in a home aquarium provided it is at least 50cm (20in) long. Feed them on small invertebrates, which can also be caught with a fine-meshed net. Simply swish it through muddy water and rinse off the small animals into a bucket for transfer to the tank. Put one male in the tank and two or three females to prevent the male bullying a single mate.

● Provide plenty of weed for the male to use for cover and nest materials, and keep the tank in a well-lit but cool spot. Return any young fish to the wild soon after hatching.

The smooth newt

On spring nights, shallow ponds and pools may be transformed into miniature theatres as smooth newts gather to perform elaborate courtship rituals. Glowing with colour, males compete to impress the females.

Large black spots all over its brownish green body, and a stripey nose, identify the male smooth newt.

Newts and their close relatives, the salamanders, occur all over the world. There are 16 species of newt in Europe but only three are native to Britain – the smooth, palmate and geat crested newts. Of these, the smooth newt is the commonest, occurring throughout much of the country.

Like all amphibians, smooth newts must return to water to breed, but they are only semi-aquatic, spending some six to ten months of the year on land. This means they can make use of ponds that may dry up temporarily. Even so, continued land drainage has undoubtedly contributed to the gradual decline of the British population.

Spring gatherings

Smooth newts prefer shallower, less acidic water than the very similar palmate newts. Smooth newts breed in farm pools, garden ponds and secluded backwaters. The newts gather in the water from early spring to begin their mating displays. They are typically most active after dark, but they also perform in daylight when careful investigation may reveal growing numbers of males pursuing females among the weeds in sunlit pools.

Females seen on their own, especially at night between April and June, will often be searching for suitable plants on which to lay their eggs. Each female examines the leaves with her nose and lips, then uses her hind legs to conceal each egg by securing a curled leaf around the sticky capsule.

Smooth newts usually lay between three and seven eggs per day, and up to 300 in total, often on adjacent stems. The young that hatch from eggs laid before June develop into adults in the year they were laid, but any that hatch from eggs laid later than June overwinter as tadpoles before turning into adults the following spring.

Newt development is different from that of frogs and other amphibians. The main difference is that the young hatch with a full complement of body organs. The stages of development are similar in all British newt species, but the pace of devlopment is determined by the temperature of the water.

After only seven days in the egg, the newt embryo resembles the adult, complete with head, body and tail. Within a month after the eggs are laid, the young newts will have digested their own egg capsules and freed themselves. At first they appear quite uncoordinated, swimming aimlessly about until they bump into something. Adhesive organs on their skin allow them to attach themselves to anything they come into contact with, and this prevents them being swept away by water currents.

Smooth newts are given partial protection by the Wildlife and Countryside Act 1981. Unlike the great crested newt, they do not enjoy fully protected status but may not be collected or exploited commercially. Permission from local landowners is needed to take any newts from ponds.

SMOOTH NEWT FACT FILE

Despite their numbers, smooth newts are rarely seen except in spring, when they search out freshwater ponds with plenty of surrounding weeds in which to breed. The male develops patches of orange and blue on its tail, which it holds erect and waves to attract a mate.

● NAMES
Common name: smooth newt, common newt
Scientific name: *Triturus vulgaris*

● HABITAT
Shallow, weedy ponds in lowland areas; on land, dark, damp places such as under stones and logs

● DISTRIBUTION
Concentrated populations throughout British Isles

● STATUS
10 million; common but declining

● SIZE
Adults 7.5–11cm (3–4in) long including tail; males larger than females

● KEY FEATURES
Three grooves on head, dark spots on body; spots on belly usually extend to throat; sheds skin periodically

● HABITS
Breeds in shallow water; hunts in water and on land in damp places; avoids dry, sunlit areas where it could dry out and die

● VOICE
High-pitched squeak when alarmed

● FOOD
Carnivorous; eats small animals ranging from water fleas and freshwater shrimps to small slugs, earthworms and insects

● EGGS
200–300, 3mm (⅛in) across, usually cream or buff, occasionally pinkish; hatch in 1–3 weeks

● BREEDING
March–June; first breeds in third or fourth spring, when courtship colours develop on the males; small brown tadpoles difficult to distinguish from those of palmate newts

Distribution map key

Present all year round

Not present

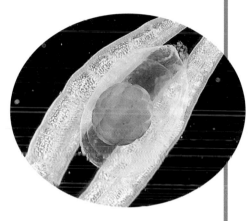

Females lay their eggs singly, rather than in clumps or strings, as frogs and toads do. Each egg is coated in jelly, attached to a water plant and carefully concealed beneath a folded leaf.

Although the thin, smooth skin becomes more leathery on land it still has to be kept damp.

Long toes provide stability when the newt moves through water or over damp ground.

Extra power in water and land is provided by the broad, flattened tail.

SPRING COURTSHIP

Between March and June male smooth newts investigate females by sniffing their cloacas. Each male pursues one female, swimming in front of her to block her way, arching his back, swishing his tail very fast against the sides of his body and releasing sexually attractive secretions. He develops an orange, yellow or red central belly stripe and a dragon-like crest that extends from the back of the head to the tail. Eventually, he drops up to three sacs of sperm on the floor of the pond in front of the female. She presses her genital slit on to one of these packages and takes up the sperm to fertilise her eggs.

Pale-bellied females are sniffed and pursued by the more strongly marked males as soon as they arrive in the pond.

At this stage the embryonic newts are only about 7mm (⅛in) long, and pale green or brown. Their skin is almost transparent and it is possible to see blood flowing around their gills and fins. The forelimbs start to appear after 10 days, followed by long, spindly fingers. The hind limbs appear after six weeks, by which time the young newts have become proficient predators. They now have four feet to chase prey through dense cover, and a large tail for propulsion in open water. Apart from their prominent feathery gills they look like miniature versions of their parents. Eventually their gills are reabsorbed and they develop lungs, enabling them to emerge from the water and hunt on land as adults.

Food and hunting

Newts track down their food by both sight and smell, although the final attack is stimulated by movement. Any prey moving quickly through the water near the head is snapped up with astonishing precision. The newt's small teeth are aligned on both jaws and on the palate.

The fast-moving smooth newt can see and smell both in water and on land. Consequently, smooth newts are able to respond very quickly to any sudden movement in either environment.

▶ This early embryo of a smooth newt is clearly visible through the transparent jelly of the egg capsule. The head and body are already distinct and the gills are a small spike behind the head.

▼ A newt tadpole digests its egg capsule as it hatches, providing it with a vital first meal. Apart from their pale skins, newt tadpoles resemble frog tadpoles, but they are more highly developed and feed exclusively on other small animals.

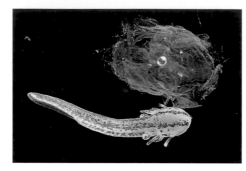

However, the teeth are adapted for gripping rather than chewing, so food is swallowed whole.

Newt tadpoles eat crustaceans, usually water fleas, until they can manage larger prey. Sometimes they eat each other. The adults will devour anything they can catch, from worms and insects on land, to aquatic snails (eaten whole) and frog tadpoles in the water. They seem to have no concept of size when they attack, and they sometimes tackle prey that is much too large for them, occasionally causing them to choke. In turn, newt tadpoles are eaten by many of the larger pond species, including most fish, but adult newts seem to be ignored by most predators.

It is rare to see anything of the lives of these secretive animals other than during their underwater courtship. When the breeding season has ended for the adults,

▼ At four to six weeks the smooth newt tadpole loses its adhesive organs and swims freely in search of food. It obtains oxygen from the water through the feathery gills behind its head.

or in autumn when the tadpoles have absorbed their gills, they slip away overnight. Travelling overland, they search for food and protective cover. In mid-winter, when they develop a thicker, velvety skin, they hibernate underground or beneath rocks and logs. The orange belly indicates their species but otherwise they are drab brown in appearance. In April they reappear and creep through the undergrowth, relying on their sense of smell to guide them back to a pond.

WILDLIFE WATCH

How can I encourage smooth newts?

● The best way to attract newts is to create a pond with suitable conditions for them to breed. Newts will often quickly colonise of their own accord.

● Pondside vegetation provides important protection for newts. They also need piles of logs or stones to shelter them from frosts during hibernation.

● An ideal pond should have gently sloping banks, shallow sunlit areas for feeding, open water for courtship and deeper areas to provide refuge in cold spring weather.

● Avoid using garden chemicals and fertilisers and don't put fish in the pond, because they will eat newt tadpoles.

● Lift excess silt and vegetation in autumn – leave it on the banks for 24 hours to allow any resident animals to depart before removing it for compost.

● For further information on managing newt habitats contact Froglife at White Lodge, London Road, Peterborough PE7 0LG (telephone 01733 558 844) or visit www.froglife.org

LIFE ON LAND

On land, smooth newts must shelter in moist places, often under stones or logs, or in damp vegetation such as garden compost heaps. This is because their skin is so thin that oxygen can diffuse through it – in effect they breathe through their skin and through the lining of their mouths. In the open, especially in warm air, they are in danger of drying out.

Newts emerge at night and on damp days to search for food, such as slugs, worms and insects, but rarely venture far from their hiding places. Occasionally, they return to their 'home' pond out of season.

For the winter, they find damp but frost-free hideaways. The body temperature of a newt varies according to its surroundings, so it drops as the air temperature falls, rendering the animal torpid and inactive. It can stay in this state, without the need for food, until the weather improves.

A smooth newt rarely emerges from under its stone in dry weather. Its elongated shape means that a relatively large surface area is exposed to the drying effects of moving air.

Recognising frogs and toads

In ponds and ditches, frogs and toads awake from winter hibernation to announce their presence, the deep croak of the common frog mingling with the high-pitched calls of the common toad.

As temperatures rise in the spring, frogs and toads emerge from their winter hibernation to feed and sit in the sun. Soon they will be heading for their breeding ponds where they will spawn and spend the rest of the summer.

The tiny tree frog has suction pads on its toes, which enables it to climb among vegetation.

Four species are native to the British Isles – the common frog, the pool frog, the common toad and the natterjack toad. Of these the pool frog is probably extinct in the wild and the natterjack toad is very rare, despite having the longest breeding season of all the species. It can still be found on a few southern heaths and coastal pools in Norfolk, north-western England and south-western Ireland. However, the appropriately named common frog and common toad are to be found all over the country.

Although not native, the marsh frog, the largest of all European frogs, has long been established in southern England, as has the edible frog. It is illegal to release non-native creatures deliberately, but in recent years African clawed toads have escaped into a few pools in Wales. Other species that may very occasionally be found in the wild include the American bullfrog, midwife toad and, on Jersey only, the agile frog. European tree frog colonies, however, have probably all died out, although these frogs may still be seen in captivity. Despite its name, the tree frog is more closely related to toads than it is to frogs.

Common toads and common frogs often share the same breeding pools. Frogs and toads frequently live in mixed colonies and may even try to mate with one another, unsuccessfully.

WILDLIFE WATCH

Where can I see frogs and toads?

● Adult frogs and toads are easiest to see in early spring. Look for croaking males in the shallows and mating pairs producing spawn among the water plants.

● By midsummer, most adult frogs and toads will be on dry land close to the spawning ponds.

EASY GUIDE TO SPOTTING FROGS AND TOADS

Common frog *Marsh frog* *Pool frog* *Edible frog*

Tree frog *Common toad* *Natterjack toad* *African clawed toad*

WHAT ARE FROGS AND TOADS?

● Frogs and toads are squat-bodied animals with long hind limbs. They are amphibians, belonging to the order Anura, meaning 'no tail', and are sometimes referred to as anurans.

● Adult frogs and toads are able to live both in water and on land. The time spent in these two very different environments varies from species to species. All frogs and toads found in the British Isles must return to water to spawn.

Distribution map key

 Present   Not present

HOW CAN I IDENTIFY FROGS AND TOADS?

● Body colour, head shape and markings are important in differentiating between frogs and toads. Frogs generally have streamlined bodies and smooth, wet skins. Toads have plump, compact bodies and dry, warty skins.

● Toads have shorter legs than frogs. On land, toads tend to walk with a shuffling movement although they hop when alarmed. Their leaps are not nearly as long as the prodigious leaps of frogs.

● To distinguish the common toad from the natterjack, look for the latter's dorsal stripe. Both species favour still waters.

● The introduced African clawed toad has a flattened body and webbed hind feet.

COMMON FROG *Rana temporaria*

In the breeding season, the male looks rather flabby and has a bluish tinge with a bluish grey throat and dark thickened pads on the thumbs to help him grasp the much larger female during mating. When ready to spawn, the female develops pearly granules on flanks and hindlegs, which also helps the male to grip her otherwise slippery body.

The common frog is extremely variable in colour but is usually a greenish brown with darker blotches and the hint of a dark 'mask' on the face.

● SIZE
6–10cm (2½–4in) long

● BREEDING
Females lay 1000–2000 eggs in jelly-like spawn in early spring

● FOOD
Invertebrates, including beetles, flies, snails, slugs and woodlice

● HABITAT
Ponds, canals, marshes, wet woodland and meadows, moorland and gardens

● VOICE
Chorus of deep croaks from males during breeding season

In hot weather a common frog always seeks shelter, such as under the leaves of a water lily, although its moist skin provides it with a degree of protection against drying out in the sun.

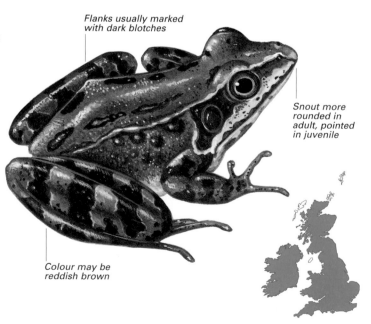

Flanks usually marked with dark blotches

Snout more rounded in adult, pointed in juvenile

Colour may be reddish brown

MARSH FROG *Rana ridibunda*

The introduced marsh frog is similar to the common frog but larger and greener, and it has no hint of a face mask. Females are bigger than males but males inflate large, grey vocal sacs on either side of the mouth in spring, when they croak loudly to attract a mate.

- **SIZE**
  9–15cm (3½–6in) long
- **BREEDING**
  Females spawn in April or May
- **FOOD**
  Mainly invertebrates
- **HABITAT**
  Deep ditches, large ponds in low-lying river valleys, usually near coast
- **VOICE**
  Loud cackling calls from males during breeding season, after dark and often in chorus

A marsh frog suns itself on floating aquatic vegetation. These frogs stay near water all year and disappear beneath the surface when alarmed.

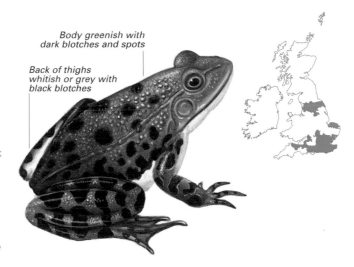

Body greenish with dark blotches and spots

Back of thighs whitish or grey with black blotches

POOL FROG *Rana lessonae*

Together with the marsh frog and the edible frog, the pool frog is often referred to as a green frog, although its body colour is mostly olive brown or bronze. It has dark blotches and a pale stripe running along the back. Males have similar vocal sacs to marsh frogs, which they inflate in spring.

- **SIZE**
  6–8cm (2½–3¼in) long
- **BREEDING**
  Females spawn in March–April
- **FOOD**
  Mainly invertebrates
- **HABITAT**
  Found in or near ponds
- **VOICE**
  Croaks of males less resonant and more even than those of marsh frogs; can sound like the quacking of ducks

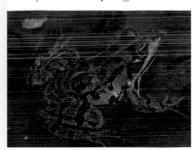

Marginally smaller than the common frog, the pool frog has a more heavily patterned body and its colour is variable.

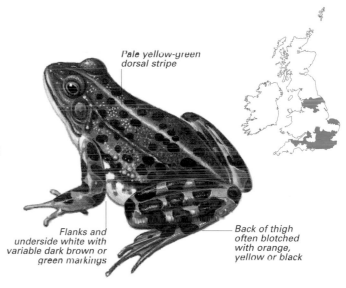

Pale yellow-green dorsal stripe

Flanks and underside white with variable dark brown or green markings

Back of thigh often blotched with orange, yellow or black

EDIBLE FROG *Rana kl. esculenta*

Once regarded as a distinct species, the edible frog is now known to be a hybrid between the pool frog and the marsh frog. Its colour varies greatly but it usually has a bright yellow or greenish back stripe. The back of the thigh is blotched black and orange.

- **SIZE**
  8–12cm (3¼–4½in) long
- **BREEDING**
  Females spawn in May or early June
- **FOOD**
  Mainly invertebrates
- **HABITAT**
  Small ponds, canals, ditches and gravel pits
- **VOICE**
  Loud, staccato mating calls; other calls quieter

The edible frog never strays far from water, although it may bask on sunny banks. In winter it hibernates in the mud at the bottom of shallow pools.

Body colour often green but ranges through olive to brown

Male's vocal sacs appear white or grey when inflated

Back of thighs often marked with orange

EUROPEAN (OR COMMON) TREE FROG *Hyla arborea*

This strikingly marked frog was introduced from southern Europe. It climbs among waterside vegetation, although not necessarily in trees. Its bright green colour affords it good camouflage, and suckers on the toes keep it secure. When expanded, its single vocal sac almost doubles the frog's size.

● SIZE
4–5cm (1½–2in) long

● BREEDING
Females lay up to 800 eggs in floating oval masses

● FOOD
Mainly nocturnal insects

● HABITAT
Any well-vegetated location with a sunny pool, including gardens and open woodland

● VOICE
Remarkably loud calls from males at night during breeding season; distinctive *'krak krak krak'* likened to a duck's quack or a small dog's bark

Until it moves, the tree frog can be difficult to spot, even when it is resting on vegetation that does not match its body colour. It is now thought to be extinct in the wild in Britain.

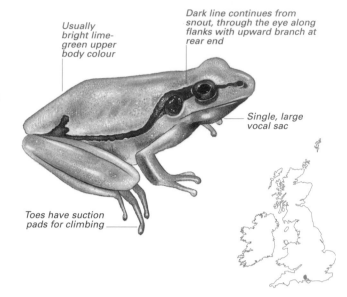

Usually bright lime-green upper body colour

Dark line continues from snout, through the eye along flanks with upward branch at rear end

Single, large vocal sac

Toes have suction pads for climbing

COMMON TOAD *Bufo bufo*

Extremely variable in colour, the common toad is usually olive brown, dull greenish or greyish. Its underside is creamy white or grey, often with dark marbling. Its skin, which is dry and knobbly, releases a toxin to deter predators. Outside the breeding season, the species often hides under logs, emerging at night to feed. If attacked, the common toad adopts a threat posture, standing up on all four legs.

● SIZE
Males 5–6cm (2–2½in) long; females 8–9cm (3¼–3½in) long or more

● BREEDING
Females lay eggs in long strings, usually double rows, of jelly-like spawn twined around pond weed

● FOOD
Invertebrates including beetles, ants, spiders, earwigs, snails, slugs and earthworms

● HABITAT
Ponds in spring, rest of year in woodland, gardens, meadows and other relatively dry places

● VOICE
Fairly high-pitched croaking from males during breeding season

The common toad's large eyes are placed on top of its head and give good all-round vision.

For the first few years of its adult life, the common toad stays away from water, visiting a pond only during a dry spell. It returns when it is ready to breed.

Conspicuously warty skin

Beady eye has golden or copper-coloured iris

Legs suited to walking on land and swimming

NATTERJACK TOAD *Bufo calamita*

Common in warm, Mediterranean countries, the natterjack toad is on the northern edge of its range in Britain. Smaller than the common toad, its upperparts are more mottled and it usually has a narrow stripe running all the way down its back. Its body also looks more flattened than the common toad's and its skin is covered with large warts. The natterjack toad often runs in short bursts, rather than walking or hopping. It is most active at night, especially after thundery rain.

● SIZE
6–8cm (2½–3¼in) long but rarely more than 7.5cm (2¾in)

● BREEDING
Females lay eggs in long strings, usually single rows, between late March and early August

● FOOD
Invertebrates

● HABITAT
Sandy lowland heaths and coastal dunes where the climate is mild and the soil loose enough for them to dig their burrows

● VOICE
Incessant, very loud, high-pitched croak from males in breeding season

Short legs result in fast, shuffling walk or run on land

Conspicuous dorsal stripe

Golden eyes have horizontal pupils

Natterjack toads are essentially nocturnal, except just after they emerge from hibernation. In summer, they hide away during particularly hot, dry weather.

AFRICAN CLAWED TOAD *Xenopus laevis*

A tropical species, the African clawed toad is sometimes kept as a pet or in laboratories, but is very rare in the wild and now found only in one small area of Wales. It is also known as the African clawed frog or platanna. Its streamlined body is as fast and agile in the water as any fish. A lateral line that runs along each side of the body, resembling a row of stitches in a wound, contains organs that can sense movement. This toad rarely ventures out of water. It is nocturnal and very secretive.

● SIZE
Up to 12cm (4½in) long

● BREEDING
Each female lays 10,000 or more eggs during the summer

● FOOD
Invertebrates as well as small fish and other amphibians; may eat its own tadpoles; takes dead as well as live animals

● HABITAT
Has survived when released into both flowing and still waters

● VOICE
Hard to hear, calls underwater

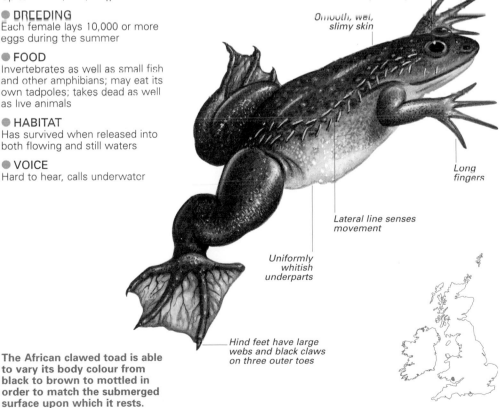

Eyes right on top of head point skyward

Smooth, wet, slimy skin

Long fingers

Lateral line senses movement

Uniformly whitish underparts

Hind feet have large webs and black claws on three outer toes

The African clawed toad is able to vary its body colour from black to brown to mottled in order to match the submerged surface upon which it rests.

Mayflies

The final few hours of a mayfly's life make a vivid contrast with the rest of its existence, as it emerges from the depths of the river bed to dance through the air in the bright sunshine.

Spring is mayfly season on the river. Few insects are as aptly named as these apparently short-lived creatures, which swarm over rivers and streams in the latter half of May and early June, but become much less common as summer advances. They are famous for living for just a day, but this is misleading. Their existence as winged adults certainly is fleeting, but each insect lives for a year or even two years, depending on species, spending its entire life apart from the last few hours as an aquatic larva, or nymph.

Unlike stoneflies, caddis flies and lacewings, adult mayflies hold their wings vertically aloft over their backs when they are perched on waterside vegetation. There are eight families and 47 species in Britain and Ireland, all of which lay their eggs in rivers and still waters.

Aquatic nymphs

The mayfly life cycle starts with the eggs, which in most species are scattered on the water surface from late spring to early autumn. These drift down through the water until they land on the bottom of the stream. Here they hatch into tiny nymphs, which burrow into the silt, crawl among submerged plants, or cling to stones in fast-flowing streams. The nymphs must hide from bottom-feeding fish, such as barbel and carp, and diving ducks.

Very little water flows through their hiding places, so each nymph must keep pumping oxygenated water over its gills to survive. It must also keep its hiding place clear of debris. However, much of this contains food in the form of algae, decaying plant and animal remains, and the fungi and bacteria that break them down. The nymph feeds by eating the debris and extracting any nutrients. It has to eat most of the time to develop through a series of stages, known as instars, shedding its skin each time as it grows larger. It must also eat for the future, because all the nutrients that it will need as a winged adult must be eaten during the nymph stage – adult mayflies have greatly reduced mouthparts and cannot feed.

An adult common mayfly, unable to fold its wings along its body, holds them high above its back in a characteristic pose. Despite their large wings, mayflies have a weak, fluttering flight.

This pond olive nymph displays the three-pronged tail that is a distinctive feature of all mayfly nymphs, distinguishing them from the nymphs of the stonefly, damselfly and dragonfly.

ANGLER'S MAYFLIES

The most familiar mayflies belong to the family Ephemeridae. Three of these species are found in the British Isles and are imitated by anglers in pursuit of fish – *Ephemera danica* (the green drake or angler's 'mayfly'), the largest British species, found in lakes and gravel-bedded rivers, the less common *Ephemera vulgata* found usually in muddy rivers, and *Ephemera lineata*, a large, river species.

Other mayflies used by fly fishermen as models for artifical flies include the small dark olive, iron blue and pale watery (*Baetis* species), the blue-winged olive (*Ephemerella ignita*), the spurwings (*Centroptilum* species) and the very small angler's curse (*Caenis* species).

◀ The larvae of most species take a year to grow to full size underwater, but some species take two years. They feed on tiny edible particles and obtain oxygen through large feathery gills.

▼ A diving duck searches for food. These ducks depend on mayfly larvae and similar bottom-dwelling insects to provide a substantial part of their protein requirement.

The nymphs live like this for one or two years, growing into fat yellow or brownish larvae that can number many hundreds per square metre (square yard) on suitably rich, silty lake or river beds. They can sense water temperatures and day lengths, timing their maturation so they emerge together, hatch into adult flies, mate and lay the next generation of eggs. The nymphs swim to the surface, struggle to escape from their tight nymphal skins, and wait on the surface while their wings harden. This is a very risky time for these large, juicy insects, because they are extremely vulnerable to predators, such as trout, river birds including wagtails and dippers, and Daubenton's bats.

The newly emerged sub-imagos or 'duns' are drab-looking, waxy-skinned insects, but after a few hours they shed their final skins to emerge as shiny imagos, or 'spinners'. Mayflies are unique among insects in moulting after they reach the winged phase in their life.

The spinners take to the air, heading upwind in large groups, the males dancing in order to entice ripe females to join the swarm and mate. After mating, the males fall back to the water, spinning round and round, which explains their name. Coupled flies also drift downwards but break their embrace before reaching the water or ground. Mated females retreat to bankside bushes, allowing time for all their eggs to be fertilised, before returning to the river to shed them. Then they too fall flat-winged on the surface. Meanwhile, the 2000–3000 eggs laid by each female sink to the river bed, and the cycle starts again.

WILDLIFE WATCH

Where can I see mayflies?

● Most rivers, chalk streams and still waters attract mayflies. The peak annual mayfly hatch usually occurs during the last two weeks of May and the first week of June, but adults of various species can be seen on the wing from February to November. Mayflies start hatching from late morning onwards. The nymphs swim up to the surface (often chased by hungry fish) and discard their nymphal case in the surface film. The emerged sub-imagos fly off weakly to hide before undergoing another moult to produce winged adults. Later in the day, mated females can often be seen returning to the river to lay their eggs and falling on to the water surface to die. They sometimes mistake wet roads for rivers and lay their eggs on them instead. Windy weather can also be a hazard to these fairly weak-flying insects, sweeping them off course and away from the river.

● Mayfly nymphs live on the river bed and can be caught in a stout, fine-meshed net in early spring. Choose a firm-bedded stream and don't go alone, for safety reasons. Also be sure to return the catch to the water. Wade into the water, hold the net downstream, close to the bottom, and shuffle your feet vigorously. Many invertebrates will be dislodged and swept into the net, which can then be emptied into some clean water in a white plastic tray. Mayfly nymphs are large and pale-bodied with feathery gills flanking their abdomens. If mayflies are plentiful there may be two sizes of nymph. These will be one and two-year-olds of long-lived species.

▶ When mayflies first emerge from the water, the soft-bodied insects are vulnerable to spiders among other predators. At this stage, their wings are screwed up in buds but they soon expand and stiffen in the air.

▼ Mated females rest in the shelter of waterside vegetation before they fly back to the river to lay their eggs, and then die.

Aquatic plants

Some plants that are specially adapted to living in water grow wholly submerged, their tiny flowers often unnoticed as a result. Others produce showy blooms that float on the surface amid a welter of flat, dark green leaves.

Almost all stretches of water contain a few plants, and some streams and rivers support a rich flora, both along the banks and in open water. True aquatic plants root and float in water, in some cases bearing leaves and flowers that live entirely beneath the surface.

Many different flowering plant families are represented among the numerous water plants that are commonly found in Britain. For example, the water-lilies, hornworts, waterworts, mare's-tails, water-milfoils and water-starworts each belong to a different family.

One highly specialised family of aquatic plants is the Lemnaceae, or duckweeds. Each plant consists of a tiny circular leaflike disc that floats on the surface of the water.

It has a single root hanging from it, weighted by the swelling at its lower end. In warm weather duckweed rapidly multiplies and can soon form a blanket over the water. It is a favourite food of ducks – hence its name – and this helps to keep it in check.

Living in water

Water plants have long, often weak stems that reach up towards the light filtering through the surface layer. Submerged leaves are often narrow or finely divided into feathery segments that move with the current.

The leaves and stems of aquatic plants do not have the waxy skin and hairs that protect land plants from drying out. This enables gases to be absorbed and excreted all over the surface of the

submerged plant, and the minute pores that allow for gas exchange in land plants are largely absent.

Rigid conducting tissues are also much reduced. The roots, stems and leaves are hollow or spongy so that oxygen can penetrate all parts of the plant. The roots, which may be buried in almost airless mud, are adapted to living with low levels of oxygen.

Water plants either live entirely submerged, or with some parts protruding from the water – as in the so-called 'emergents'. Flowers may be large and showy or massed in spikes and borne above the surface of the water, or they may be tiny, inconspicuous and submerged. In this case, pollen transfer has to be via water rather than by insects or the wind as in land plants.

▲ Like all green plants, water-starwort uses sunlight to make carbohydrate from carbon dioxide and water. Bubbles of oxygen, a by-product of the process, are gradually released into the water.

▼ The nutrient-rich mud and slow-flowing water of the Norfolk Broads provide ideal growing conditions for the white water-lily.

AQUATIC PLANTS FACT FILE

● White water-lily
Nymphaea alba
Habitat and distribution
Ponds, lakes, canals and slow-flowing rivers, especially where bottom is muddy; widespread but absent from most of south-western England, parts of northern England and most of the southern half of Ireland
Size Stems 1–3m (3–10ft) long
Key features
Massive rootstock; floating leaves 12–35cm (4¾–14in) across, nearly circular with deep narrow cleft, held on long, hollow stalks; fragrant flowers 9–20cm (3½–8in) across, white, stamens yellow; fruit globular
Flowering time
June–September

● Yellow water-lily or brandy-bottle
Nuphar lutea
Habitat and distribution
Still and slow-flowing water, most common in rivers of central and southern England, absent from northern Scotland and most of south-western England
Size Stems 1–5m (3–16ft) long
Key features
Massive, branched rootstock; floating leaves 10–40cm (4–16in) across, oval with a deep narrow cleft or submerged and cabbage-like, on long, hollow stalks; flowers 5–8cm (2–3in) across, cup shaped, yellow; flask-shaped fruit smells slightly of brandy
Flowering time
June–September

● Least water-lily
Nuphar pumila
Habitat and distribution
Still, sheltered waters of pools and small rivers in Scottish Highlands and meres of north Shropshire
Size Stems 0.5–2.5m (1ft 6in–8ft 2in) long
Key features
Similar to yellow water-lily, but much smaller; flowers 1.5–3.5cm (⅝–1⅜in) across; hybridises with yellow water-lily to form plants that are intermediate in appearance and may occur away from both parents
Flowering time
July–August

● Rigid hornwort
Ceratophyllum demersum
Habitat and distribution
Still and slow-flowing waters; rare in south-west England, Wales, northern Scotland and Ireland
Size 30–150cm (1–5ft) tall
Key features
Leaves submerged, brittle, in whorls of 3–8, crowded towards stem tips, forked into narrow segments; flowers tiny, green, often not appearing; fruits 5mm (¼in) long, beaked with 2 basal spines
Flowering time
July–September

● Soft hornwort
Ceratophyllum submersum
Habitat and distribution
Ponds, ditches and canals, especially near the sea; mainly in south-east England and an area from the Midlands to south Wales
Size 20–80cm (8–32in) tall
Key features
Submerged, similar to rigid hornwort, but leaves softer, paler green; fruit without basal spines
Flowering time
July–September

Least water-lily
Nuphar pumila

Yellow water-lily or brandy-bottle
Nuphar lutea

White water-lily
Nymphaea alba

Soft hornwort
Ceratophyllum submersum

Rigid hornwort
Ceratophyllum demersum

 DANGER!
Water is always hazardous and its depth can be unpredictable. Watch out for slippery and unstable banks, deep mud and underwater objects, such as broken bottles. Water plants themselves pose a threat to swimmers, easily entangling arms and legs.

The white water-lily can be found in ponds and lakes, where its elegant, pale blooms open from June to September.

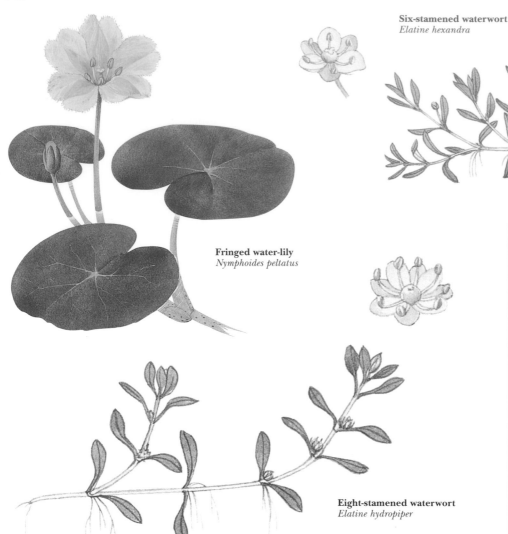

Fringed water-lily
Nymphoides peltatus

Six-stamened waterwort
Elatine hexandra

Eight-stamened waterwort
Elatine hydropiper

The bogbean is more attractive than its name suggests. In the Middle Ages it was used as a cure for scurvy and rheumatism while the Irish thought that it purified the blood. Its dried leaves have also been used in herbal tobacco.

Bogbean or buckbean
Menyanthes trifoliata

AQUATIC PLANTS FACT FILE

● **Fringed water-lily**
Nymphoides peltatus
Habitat and distribution
Still and slow-flowing waters, native in the Fens and Thames Valley, but widely introduced in England and Wales
Size Stems up to 1.5m (5ft) long
Key features
Member of the bogbean family; superficially similar to yellow water-lily but leaves all floating, much smaller, shallowly toothed, purple below; flowers 3–4cm (1¼–1½in) across, petals fringed, bright yellow
Flowering time
June–September

● **Bogbean or buckbean**
Menyanthes trifoliata
Habitat and distribution
Upland lakes, boggy pools and wet marshes, on muddy and peaty soils; more common in north and west and Norfolk
Size Stems up to 1.5m (5ft) long
Key features
Leaves held in threes, raised above the water; flowers in tall, showy spikes, the petals fringed, white, pink outside
Flowering time
May–June

● **Six-stamened waterwort**
Elatine hexandra
Habitat and distribution
Margins of peaty pools and lake shores, on bare mud or submerged in shallows; scattered in the west and north, western and northern Ireland, heaths in southern England
Size Stems 2–20cm (¾–8in) long
Key features
Creeping and rooting annual or short-lived perennial; leaves in opposite pairs, narrowly elliptical, often reddish; flowers minute
Flowering time
June–September

● **Eight-stamened waterwort**
Elatine hydropiper
Habitat and distribution
Often submerged, occasionally on bare mud; very rare, found only in parts of central Scotland, Anglesey, the Severn/Wye area and north-eastern Ireland
Size Stems 2–15cm (¾–6in) long
Key features
Creeping stems, similar to six-stamened waterwort but leaves narrower at base; flowers stalkless, pink
Flowering time July–August

AQUATIC PLANTS FACT FILE

● **Common water-starwort**
Callitriche stagnalis
Habitat and distribution
Widespread, often abundant in streams, lakes and ponds, especially in lime-rich waters
Size Stems up to 60cm (2ft) long in water and 15cm (6in) on mud
Key features
Trails in water or sprawls on bare mud; stems weak and elliptical; leaves pale green, those uppermost form floating rosettes; tiny, green, 4-lobed flowers; fruit broadly winged, pale brown
Flowering time
April–October

● **Various-leaved or long-styled water-starwort**
Callitriche platycarpa
Habitat and distribution
Widespread but scattered in shallow pools, streams and ditches; sometimes grows in brackish waters
Size Stems up to 1m (3ft) long
Key features
Often prostrate, similar to common water-starwort, but leaves narrower, darker green, those submerged have almost parallel sides, brown; fruits broadly winged
Flowering time
April–October

● **Blunt-fruited water-starwort**
Callitriche obtusangula
Habitat and distribution
Widespread but local in lime-rich still waters; mainly in south-east, but as far north as Edinburgh, also in north-east of Northern Ireland
Size Stems spreading, up to 60cm (2ft) long, often shorter
Key features
Leaves narrowly diamond-shaped, yellowish green and rather fleshy; fruit unwinged, brown
Flowering time
May–July

● **Autumnal water-starwort**
Callitriche hermaphroditica
Habitat and distribution
Widespread in nutrient-rich ponds, lakes, streams and canals in northern Britain and Northern Ireland, southern outposts in Worcestershire and Co. Kerry
Size Stems up to 50cm (20in) long
Key features
All leaves submerged, up to 2cm (¾in) long, narrow, tapering to notched tip, yellowish green, translucent; fruit usually broadly winged near tip
Flowering time
May–September

● **Short-leaved water-starwort**
Callitriche truncata
Habitat and distribution
Shallow lakes, reservoirs, streams, ditches and gravel pits, sometimes in brackish water, in southern and central England, mostly in east Midlands; in only a few places elsewhere
Size Up to 20cm (8in) tall
Key features
Similar to autumnal water-starwort, but stems often reddish and more slender; leaves bluish green, 1cm (½in) long; fruit unwinged
Flowering time
May–September

● **Intermediate water-starwort**
Callitriche hamulata
Habitat and distribution
Widespread, mostly in acidic waters in lakes and slow-flowing rivers and streams
Size Up to 50cm (20in) tall
Key features
Floating leaves dark green, elliptical, submerged ones narrow with spanner-shaped notched tips; fruit narrowly winged, black
Flowering time
April–September

Common water-starwort
Callitriche stagnalis

Blunt-fruited water-starwort
Callitriche obtusangula

Short-leaved water-starwort
Callitriche truncata

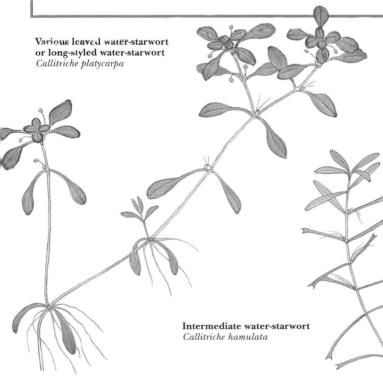

Various-leaved water-starwort
or long-styled water-starwort
Callitriche platycarpa

Intermediate water-starwort
Callitriche hamulata

Autumnal water-starwort
Callitriche hermaphroditica

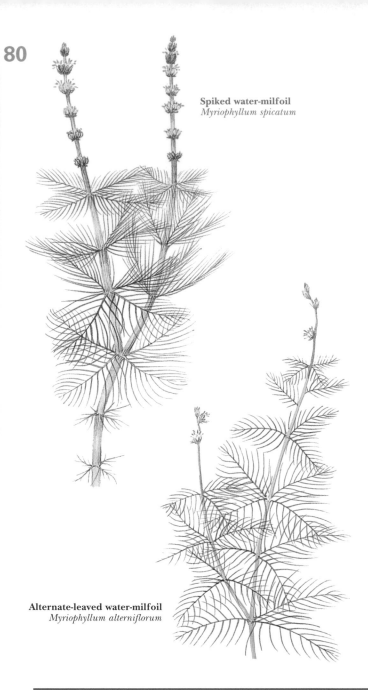

Spiked water-milfoil
Myriophyllum spicatum

Alternate-leaved water-milfoil
Myriophyllum alterniflorum

AQUATIC PLANTS FACT FILE

● **Spiked water-milfoil**
Myriophyllum spicatum
Habitat and distribution
Widespread, mainly in lowlands, in still or slow-flowing mainly lime-rich, sometimes brackish, waters
Size Stems 2.5m (8ft 2in) long
Key features
Leaves in whorls of 4, sometimes 5, much divided, feathery; flowers inconspicuous, greenish yellow or reddish in erect, almost leafless spikes emerging from water; fruits with small swellings
Flowering time
June–September

● **Alternate-leaved water-milfoil**
Myriophyllum alterniflorum
Habitat and distribution
Mostly in peaty, acidic, still or slow-flowing waters; scattered throughout the British Isles, but mainly in west and north; rare in central England
Size Stems up to 1m (3ft) long, often shorter
Key features
Similar to spiked water-milfoil but more slender, leaves shorter, less divided, few-flowered spikes of yellowish flowers that droop in bud
Flowering time
May–August

● **Whorled water-milfoil**
Myriophyllum verticillatum
Habitat and distribution
Widespread but scattered in ponds, ditches and lakes with lime-rich water, mainly in southern half of England, southern Wales and parts of Ireland; not in Scotland
Size Stems up to 3m (10ft) long
Key features
Similar to spiked water-milfoil but leaves usually in whorls of 5, flowers greenish, with feathery bracts at base; fruits smooth
Flowering time
July–August

● **Mare's-tail**
Hippuris vulgaris
Habitat and distribution
Widespread, except for south-western England, much of Wales, northern Scotland and southern Ireland; grows in shallow lakes, ponds and slow-flowing streams
Size Up to 60cm (2ft) tall, sometimes more
Key features
A stiffer, more erect unbranched plant than the water-milfoils, with undivided strap-like, dark-green leaves in whorls of 6–12; flowers minute, pinkish, at base of leaves; fruit a tiny greenish nut
Flowering time
June–August

Whorled water-milfoil
Myriophyllum verticillatum

Mare's-tail
Hippuris vulgaris

WILDLIFE WATCH

Where can I see water plants?

● Water plants can usually be observed in any body of water, be it a farm ditch or a large lake. Some species are very localised in their distribution, reflecting their exacting requirements for certain minerals, clear water or lack of disturbance.

● The best places for water plants are still, unpolluted, natural waters fed by springs, and clean, often lime-rich streams that have not been contaminated by run-off from agricultural land. Some species require the peaty, acidic rivers and lakes of Scotland and western Ireland. Rural canals, backwaters and good-quality water – as can be found in trout streams and upland lakes – are also good places to visit in order to look for aquatic plants.

● Several water plants are robust, frequently growing in unkempt ponds or inner-city canals. Yellow water-lilies fringe many canals and rivers in central and southern England.

● Some water plants have fared particularly well in recent years. The handsome fringed water-lily, which was once restricted to the Fens and the Thames Valley, is today spreading, probably by virtue of its popularity as a hardy, ornamental plant for garden ponds – discarded plants may be colonising slow-flowing waters in the wild.

● Mare's-tail grows in the same habitat as a similar non-flowering plant with longer whorls, which are actually stems – the water horsetail.

Coast watch

- The common seal
- The avocet
- The puffin
- The shelduck
- The common lobster
- The periwinkle
- Coral
- Sea urchins
- Recognising coastal lichens
- Peaflowers

The common seal

When on land this placid mammal lazes on sand banks or seaweed-covered rocks. Once in the water, however, the common seal swims with grace and power, its excellent eyesight directing it towards unsuspecting fish.

Built for efficient swimming, the common seal's bulky body is clumsy on shore. It arches and flops as the animal tries to move and, since travelling on land is such an effort, the common seal often swims to the shallow water over sand banks and allows itself to be stranded when the tide goes out. It can then bask quietly – the common seal is not noisy even at breeding time. A sand bank also gives the seal a useful look-out position. If disturbed, it shuffles back into the water, but often returns to the same place every day.

The common, or harbour, seal is the seal most often found in cold to temperate waters throughout the northern hemisphere. However, it is less numerous around Britain than its larger relative, the Atlantic grey seal, and generally swims in more northerly seas. About 90 per cent of both seals in Britain live around Scotland. Unlike the grey seal, the common seal does not live in an organised herd. It is not a sociable animal, although groups of more than 100 sometimes choose the same place to lie in the sun.

Swimming in cold seas

The seal's body wobbles as it tries to move on land because of the thick layer of blubber that both streamlines and insulates its body. This layer of blubber amounts to around 60 per cent of the seal's body weight – in comparison, the fat on a fit human amounts to 15–20 per cent of body weight. The seal's blubber keeps its internal body temperature high enough for its brain and muscles to function efficiently. While in the water, the outer layers of blubber ripple into corrugations, trapping pockets of water against the skin. This makes the seal more hydrodynamic, because water slips easily over the layer of water trapped against its skin as it swims.

Unlike its relatives the sea lion and walrus, which use their forelimbs to propel their bodies through water, the common seal's forelimbs are just for manoeuvring. The seal uses its hind flippers for swimming, employing an inward stroke powered by its back muscles. Like other true seals, it cannot swing its hind flippers forwards to help it move more easily on land, as sea lions and walruses do.

Large, forward-facing eyes allow the common seal to see well both on land and under water.

COMMON SEAL FACT FILE

A rounded, dog-like head and short muzzle distinguish the common seal from the long-headed Atlantic grey seal. The common seal also favours more sheltered waters than its larger cousin.

● **NAMES**
Common names: harbour or common seal
Scientific name: *Phoca vitulina*

● **HABITAT**
Around sheltered shores and estuaries

● **DISTRIBUTION**
Coasts of Wales, Ireland, Scotland (including the Isles) and England, mainly in the Wash, as far south as the Thames estuary

● **STATUS**
Estimated 50,000–60,000 around British Isles (more than 85% around Scotland)

● **SIZE**
Males 130–195cm (4ft 4in–6ft 6in) long; females 120–155cm (4ft–5ft 2in) long; weight 45–130kg (99–287lb)

● **KEY FEATURES**
Smaller than grey seal, head more rounded; nostrils 'V'-shaped. Mottled with pale greyish, dark brown or black spots on similar background; moults annually

● **HABITS**
Feeds and mates at sea; inactive on shore

● **FOOD**
Fish, both bottom-dwelling and mid-water, some squid, molluscs and crustaceans

● **BREEDING**
Single pups born in June or July; rarely twins

● **NEST**
Females give birth among rocks or on sandy beach

● **YOUNG**
White puppy fur often shed before birth; swim shortly after birth; suckled for 3–6 weeks

Common seals have been legally protected by the Conservation of Seals Act since 1970. They may not be killed around British coasts between 1 June and 31 August without a licence.

Distribution map key

■ Present all year round
□ Not present

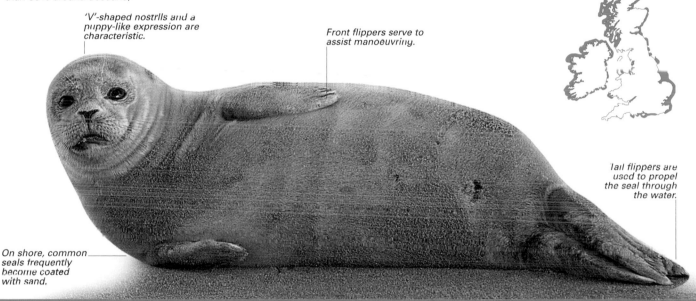

'V'-shaped nostrils and a puppy-like expression are characteristic.

Front flippers serve to assist manoeuvring.

Tail flippers are used to propel the seal through the water.

On shore, common seals frequently become coated with sand.

The common seal tends to leave the water only in secluded locations. Vulnerable on land, it is quick to slip back into the sea at the slightest sign of danger.

Seafood diet

Adult common seals feed mainly on fish, such as cod, herring, mackerel and flatfish. They need to eat at least 1–3kg (2–6½lb) a day, so they prey upon whatever is available. They eat small fish whole but grip larger fish in their front flippers, tearing them up with the claws on the flippers and their teeth.

Common seals normally make feeding dives of about five minutes duration, but they can remain underwater for nearly half an hour. They dive to at least 50m (165ft) and can manage up to 200m (650ft) or more. If making shallower dives, they can continue to do so for hours. Their heart-rate, which is about 120 beats per minute at the surface, drops to about 40 underwater to conserve energy. Seals have a relatively larger volume of blood than land animals so that they accumulate more

oxygen in their blood to sustain them when diving. Their muscles also have more oxygen-storing capacity than those of land animals.

Raising pups

The testes of the male are, unusually for a mammal, internal, to ensure that sperm development takes place at the best possible temperature, and to create a streamlined body for minimal water resistance. Like some other mammals, male seals have a bone in the penis. The seals mate in the water in July or August around Britain, a few weeks after pupping and at around moulting time, so they have a sleek new coat.

Common seals have evolved a system whereby the fertilised egg is suspended in the womb for about four months before the embryo develops. This delayed implantation ensures pups are

born during the summer when the weather is more likely to be favourable. As the breeding season approaches, pregnant females haul themselves out of the water at favourite nursery sites. Pups are born between the tide marks, on sand in estuaries or among rocks on the open shore. The white puppy fur is often shed before birth so that, when born, the pup is a wet, shiny, spindle-shaped bundle with hind flippers that seem large in proportion to the rest of its body. These flippers allow the pup to swim shortly after birth.

The pup must start suckling as soon as possible, within six hours at most. The mother helps the pup to locate a nipple by easing it into position with her front flippers. Suckling usually lasts for about 45 minutes. Eventually, the tide comes in and mother and pup take to the water. The mother's milk is rich

---

WILDLIFE WATCH

Where can I see common seals?

● Although beaches favoured by common seals are usually inaccessible, the north Norfolk coast – Blakeney Point in particular – has superb views of them. The seals can be seen from pleasure launches as well as from the landward side of the beach. Common seals can also be seen in Northern Ireland, where they breed at Strangford and Carlingford Loughs. In Scotland, they are found in the Orkneys, Shetland and the Dornoch and Moray Firths.

● For close-up views of both common and Atlantic grey seals, visit the seal sanctuaries at Gweek in Cornwall and King's Lynn in Norfolk.

● If a seal pup is discovered on a beach, leave it alone, because its mother will probably find it, but inform the local RSPCA office.

STUDYING SEALS

Seals are generally counted from the air first of all, because they use such secluded beaches. Unfortunately for scientists, the seals are very well camouflaged, particularly among rocks along the shore. Observers often resort to thermal images to give an approximate count, following up with a walk along the shore to check the air observations.

Recent research has involved tagging seals with radio transmitters. These are glued on to the fur at the back of the neck so that, when the seal surfaces, its position, the sea temperature, its maximum depth of diving, heart-rate and other important details are bounced off a satellite to a computer in a laboratory. The transmitter, which has a limited battery life, is shed with the moult.

in fat, so birth weight doubles in just over a week. This is mostly blubber to provide effective insulation. The mother continues to suckle the pup for about four weeks, losing weight because she does not feed while giving birth and suckling. Female pups become sexually mature after three to four years, and males by five or six years, although they may not gain enough social status to reproduce until several years later. Females can live for around 30 years, but males rarely survive beyond 20.

Increasing numbers

Although killer whales and sharks kill seals in other parts of their range, humans have had a far more significant effect on British common seal populations. Fur hunters sometimes took an entire season's young from several sites, and a decline in seal numbers up to the late 1960s led to successive conservation orders. Now that the seal population is thriving again, despite two outbreaks of phocine distemper virus (PDV) in 1988 and 2002, the rise in numbers has affected coastal fishermen and fish-farmers. Seals can damage nets and compete for fish stocks. A common seal may eat more than a tonne of fish a year and is attracted to fixed nets and farm enclosures. Fishery authorities complain that seals catch more fish than their own quotas in certain areas.

At protected sites, such as Blakeney Point on the north Norfolk coast, large numbers of common seals gather on shore for much of the day. Even though they appear relaxed and docile, a human observer who strays too close will induce mass panic among the animals, and they will retreat quickly to the safety of the sea.

SEAL SENSES

The seal's big brown eyes indicate efficient low-light vision. Internally, the eyes have a reflective layer to reflect on to the retinal cells what little underwater light enters the eye. These cells are all rod-shaped, giving acute sensitivity in poor light but in black and white only. Seals have no cone-shaped retinal cells, which are responsible for colour vision in good light.

The ears have no external lobes, but the perception of sound direction is enhanced by its transmission through certain bones of the skull. A mother first identifies her pup by sound, then confirms it is her own by smell.

Whiskers on the seal's upper lip and nose, and above its eyes, are directed forwards while it is hunting. A seal without whiskers is less effective at catching prey.

In the dark and murky waters in which they often swim, common seals use their whiskers to detect prey, such as fish and crabs, by touch. The seal's eyesight, which is effective underwater, also enables it to see its prey.

The avocet

A graceful wading bird, the avocet is breeding successfully in Britain and numbers are gradually increasing. In spring, pairs perform elaborate courtship rituals after which they set about building a shallow nest in which to lay their eggs.

With its contrasting black-and-white plumage, the avocet is one of Britain's most attractive wading birds. Its distinctive appearance compared with other waders makes it easy to recognise.

Slender, with long, grey-blue legs and a distinctive upcurved bill, the avocet is is now a familiar sight on England's eastern and southern coasts. Its presence is a result of successful conservation practices.

Although rarely common, the avocet once bred regularly in Britain, along the eastern coastline from the River Humber to Sussex. During the 18th and 19th centuries, however, its numbers declined. Initially, this was due to the drainage for land development of many of the estuaries, salt marshes, lagoons and shallow lakes on which the avocet lived. Later, numbers were drastically reduced by shooting. Eggs were also plundered by local people for food. By 1830, the avocet no longer bred in most of England. The last definite record of nesting avocets is in Dungeness, in Kent, in 1842.

Nearly a century elapsed before the species returned to the British Isles to breed. In 1938, two pairs nested on Tacunshin Lake in County Wexford – the only known incidence of avocets breeding in Ireland. Then, in 1941, a pair nested at Salthouse, north Norfolk, but did not breed. During the Second World War, a few attempts to encourage the avocet to return more widely to Britain were made but rarely successfully. The only recorded successful breeding of avocets during the war occurred when one pair bred in Essex in 1944.

FAMILIAR EMBLEM

With its elegant shape and striking black-and-white plumage, the avocet is familiar to millions as the emblem of the Royal Society for the Protection of Birds. The RSPB was established in 1889, but its association with the avocet did not begin until the spring of 1947, when four pairs were discovered nesting in Britain for the first time in over a century. Thanks to the efforts of the RSPB, the avocet is a great conservation success story. The bird made its first appearance as the emblem of the RSPB in 1955, when it was used on a new society tie. Since then, the image of the avocet has become synonymous with the organisation that has done so much to restore its fortunes.

AVOCET FACT FILE

When this tall, slim bird with startlingly white body and neat black cap is in flight, its wings seem to flicker black and white. On the ground, it walks briskly, often bobbing its head up and down if alarmed.

● **NAMES**
Common names: avocet, pied avocet
Scientific name: *Recurvirostra avosetta*

● **HABITAT**
Breeds mainly by saline lagoons, sometimes on salt marshes or by shallow lakes; occasional pairs nest inland; winters on estuaries and muddy inlets

● **DISTRIBUTION**
Breeds at scattered coastal sites between the Humber and Dorset, as well as at Leighton Moss RSPB reserve in north-west Lancashire; winters at coastal sites between East Anglia and Devon

● **STATUS**
Breeding population increasing slowly, with about 1000 pairs nesting annually in some 25 colonies; those that remain in England for the winter are joined by visitors from north-west Europe to swell numbers to more than 4500

● **SIZE**
Length 42–45cm (16½–18in), of which 7.5–8.5cm (3–3½in) is bill; wingspan 77–80cm (2ft 6in–2ft 8in); weight 250–300g (8¾–10½oz)

● **KEY FEATURES**
Black-and-white plumage; long, slender, black upcurved bill and long, bluish grey legs; males have longer, less curved bills than females; juveniles have dark brownish markings and greyer legs

● **HABITS**
Feeds in small groups by sweeping its bill from side to side in shallows; may swim and upend to reach prey

● **VOICE**
Little used away from breeding territory; contact call a fluty, melodious '*klute klute*' becoming harsher and more vibrant when bird is alarmed

● **FOOD**
Invertebrates, especially insects, crustaceans and worms; also shrimps, prawns, ragworms, midge larvae and occasionally small fish

● **BREEDING**
Mid-April–July, single clutch

● **NEST**
Shallow scrape on exposed ground near or even in shallow water; lined with marsh vegetation

● **EGGS**
Smooth oval, matt or glossy, brownish or pale buff with variable black spots and blotches; single clutch of usually 3 or 4 eggs laid at 1–2 day intervals; incubation 23–25 days, shared between sexes

● **YOUNG**
Fledge after 35–42 days, but remain dependent on parents for some time, varying from a few weeks to a few months; first breed at 2 years

Slender and curved, the black bill is adapted for probing watery mud.

Body plumage is white except for black wing panels.

Black wing tips are visible from above and below when the bird is in flight.

Long legs enable the avocet to wade in fairly deep water.

Feet are slightly webbed to aid swimming.

Distribution map key

Present all year round

Present during summer months

Present during winter months

Not present

PROTECTED!

The avocet is fully protected under Schedule 1 of the Wildlife and Countryside Act 1981, the European Commission's Birds Directive 1979, and the Berne Convention on European Wildlife 1983. It is illegal to interfere with the birds in any way or disturb their nests or young.

Sweeping movements

The avocet uses a rhythmic side-to-side motion as it moves its elegant bill through the water in search of small invertebrates. It prefers to feed in shallow water, although its long legs enable it to go deeper.

In clear water, an avocet uses its eyes as well as its bill to locate prey.

Making a comeback

One morning in May 1947, Lieutenant Colonel J. K. Stanford and his brother discovered three avocet nests, all with eggs, among the mortar bomb craters at Minsmere. That part of the Suffolk coast had been deliberately flooded as an anti-invasion measure against German landings during the Second World War, unwittingly creating new pools for water birds, including the avocet. Another pair was found nesting farther along the coast at Havergate Island. Both of these sites are now RSPB reserves where avocets breed and thrive. Although numbers have steadily increased, the avocet is still a rare breeding bird in Britain. There are only around 1000 breeding pairs, living mainly along the East Anglian coast.

Finding food

The avocet's favourite breeding sites are shallow, brackish or saline coastal lagoons and lakes, where invertebrates and insect larvae abound. As well as sweeping its bill through the water and sieving the ooze for food, an avocet may sometimes peck at the surface of the water, or at the muddy estuary bottom, in search of crustaceans and worms.

AVOCET CALENDAR

FEBRUARY • MARCH

More than 4500 avocets winter on estuaries in southern England, the majority in Suffolk, Dorset, Essex, Devon, Kent and Norfolk (listed in order of abundance in recent years).

APRIL • MAY

Avocets have deserted their wintering grounds and returned to nesting sites, while those birds that migrated have returned to Britain. By the end of April, many pairs are incubating eggs.

JUNE • JULY

Activity in the nesting colonies, mostly in East Anglia, is at its peak. After about three weeks, the eggs hatch and downy youngsters are herded to the water. Soon they will start to fly.

AUGUST • SEPTEMBER

Colonies are slowly abandoned and flocks form as the birds start their post-breeding moult. One-year-old birds that have not bred join the adults and young as they feed on estuarine mud.

OCTOBER • NOVEMBER

Some British-bred avocets migrate to the Mediterranean, or even Africa, for the winter, joining continental birds that pass through Britain on their way to southern wintering grounds.

DECEMBER • JANUARY

Those birds that have not migrated form wintering flocks, mainly at well-established coastal sites or estuaries in Britain. They are joined by small numbers of continental birds.

▲ Resting on one leg, the other held tucked up in its feathers, probably helps the avocet to reduce heat loss. For much of the year, the birds roost in close groups, the security of numbers allowing them to relax.

After swimming, the avocet flaps its wings vigorously to dry them. The wings, which are very long, producing powerful downbeats, lift the bird's light frame off the water easily.

To feed, avocets frequently wade belly-high into deep water. They also swim, upending like ducks to reach food on the bottom. Outside the breeding season, avocets often move to the food-rich tidal waters of river estuaries. They rarely occupy inland sites, although since 1996 a few pairs have nested beside inland water areas, including Kempton Park Reservoir in London.

For avocets to breed successfully, a plentiful food supply is vital. In summer, the amount of food available lessens as lagoon water evaporates and salinity increases. In some areas, the salt content of the water may be so high that there is no food at all. This severely affects the survival of young so that, even if breeding has been successful, avocets may manage to rear just one chick per nest.

Courtship and breeding

Avocets form colonies at suitable locations – often sandy or muddy islands. Each pair makes a shallow scrape on the ground with their breasts and feet. They line this with short pieces of marsh vegetation, which they also use to create a nest rim. When water levels rise, they add to the nest. From about mid-April, the female lays three or four eggs.

Sense of touch

In cloudy water, the avocet locates its prey by touch, skimming the surface of the mud with its highly sensitive bill tip. Despite its delicate-looking mandibles, this wader can tackle surprisingly large prey, including big worms, small molluscs and occasionally small fish.

The avocet holds its bill slightly open and sweeps the upcurved tip from side to side. A ragworm crawling over the mud is swiftly detected.

With a quick stab of its bill, the avocet plucks the ragworm from the sediment and swallows it before the mud has settled.

MATING CEREMONY

Once the avocets have arrived on their breeding grounds, pairs of birds engage in ritual behaviour that cements the pair bond. Most striking is the mating display, which always follows the same set pattern. First, both birds start preening very actively, repeatedly dipping their bills into the water. The female then adopts a static posture of invitation. Standing in shallow water, the bird lowers her head and reaches forwards so that the neck, head and bill are stretched out along the surface of the water. The male moves from side to side behind her, continuing to preen and splash water. The female remains frozen in the solicitation posture throughout his display.

The courtship may end here if one of the birds loses interest and leaves the scene, or it may turn into a full mating ceremony. This involves the male walking slowly around the female in ever-decreasing half-circles, until he is so close he has to stoop low in order to creep under her tail. He then stands beside her, splashing his bill in the water. Eventually, he mounts her with his bill open and wings raised. After mating, the male stands beside his mate and they cross bills. He then covers her back with one unfolded wing. The pair walk forward together for a short distance, before walking or running away from each other.

◄ Avocets start to form pairs in late winter. Prior to mating, pair bonds are established through elaborate courtship behaviour. The pair may stay together, sometimes for more than one season.

▲ The female indicates her receptiveness to the male by crouching with her wings spread. He mounts suddenly from the side, springing upwards with his wings lifted.

During the breeding season in particular, avocets are extremely aggressive in the defence of their feeding territories. In the early stages, up to the eggs hatching, they frequently perform belligerent ritual displays. This behaviour may establish a 'pecking order' within the colony and a feeding area around each nest. The most unusual of these displays is known as a grouping ceremony, or group dance. This is initiated by a breeding pair in dispute with another pair within the colony. The ceremony involves a number of adults gathering in a formal assembly

and creating a circle of as many as 20 birds. Threat calls from one of the avocet pairs bring this group together.

The birds gather quickly, occasionally coming from as far as 300m (1000ft) away to take part. Typically, the birds face inwards and perform a bowing display, often all moving in unison and stamping their feet or trampling in the mud. Very quickly, they form an almost

perfect circle with their bills pointed inwards and almost touching at the tips. These gatherings are often short-lived, as disputes break out and the large group disperses into smaller parties of birds that chase and threaten one another. The reasons for this elaborate display are not fully understood, but it probably establishes some sort of hierarchy among the breeding pairs of birds.

▼ Both birds help to build the nest, which may be quite meagre with no lining at all or a sizeable structure of grass stems and debris. The latter is likely only if the nest is near water and flooding is possible.

▲ An avocet chick leaves the nest within hours of hatching, the upward curve of its bill already apparent. Parent birds shepherd the chicks to water, where they are soon able to feed themselves.

WILDLIFE WATCH

Where can I see avocets?

● Almost all nesting avocets in Britain are on nature reserves. Visit these sites between late April and late June to see breeding birds. There are RSPB reserves at Titchwell in Norfolk, Minsmere and Havergate Island in Suffolk, Blacktoft Sands in East Yorkshire, Poole Harbour in Dorset, Leighton Moss in Lancashire and Elmley Marsh in Kent. For more information, telephone the RSPB on 01767 680551 or visit www.rspb.org

● Most eastern breeding sites are deserted in winter. By October, avocets will be found mainly on estuaries along the English Channel and southern North Sea coasts. Reliable sites include the Alde in Suffolk, Hamford Water in Essex, the Thames and the Medway, Poole Harbour in Dorset and the Exe and Tamar-Tavy in Devon.

● Each winter, special 'Avocet Cruises' are organised on the Exe estuary in Devon. For details, telephone the south-west region office of the RSPB on 01392 432691 or visit www.rspb.org/england/southwest/birdwatching/avocetcruises.asp

Protective parents

Once a pair of avocets has eggs or young, the parent birds defend them vigorously. They attack any intruding bird or mammal by running at it with their heads lowered and wings spread. At other times, they may edge towards the enemy, lifting and fluttering their wings. These displays are usually sufficient to drive away interlopers, even if they are many times larger than the parent birds. If the display is not successful, however, the avocets become even more aggressive, sometimes knocking down rivals and trampling them. They have even been known to fly at and strike human intruders.

In common with other waders, avocets employ the distraction display or 'broken wing trick' to protect their young from attack by predatory mammals. This entails an adult bird attracting the attention of a potential predator, such as a fox or

Exceptionally long legs may make settling on the nest an ungainly task, but they are easily folded away once the bird has lowered itself down. The breast feathers are fluffed out to bring them into contact with the chicks and eggs.

stoat, by floundering on the ground. Apparently injured and unable to fly, it draws the predator slowly away from the nest or young. Once clear of the nesting area, the adult abandons the subterfuge suddenly and flies away. During this time, the chicks lie motionless, relying upon the colouring of their downy plumage to give them camouflage on the ground. They become absolutely still as soon as the adults give alarm calls and start to move around and feed again only when they have heard the 'all clear'.

Occasionally, a colony falls prey to a predator. In recent years, colonies of avocet have been plundered by a wide range of predators, including kestrels and black-headed gulls, as well as the occasional stoat and fox.

Bad weather is also a danger during the breeding season and can result in massive loss of young. Despite these hazards, avocets are relatively long-lived and have been known to survive for up to 24 years.

Outside the breeding season, flocks of up to 30 avocets are not unusual and larger groups can build up on favoured sites on Britain's south and south-east coasts.

The puffin

Flying far out to sea and nesting mainly on remote offshore islands, the puffin rarely ventures inland except when driven ashore by exceptionally violent storms. Then this distinctive bird heads for lakes and reservoirs.

Huge numbers of puffins breed in Britain and Ireland – well over three times the number of herring gulls. Unlike these adaptable gulls, which often feed inland and breed in Britain's cities, puffins do not live inland or near humans.

For most of the year puffins live far out at sea, diving to feed on small fish and large plankton. They are efficient hunters, but rough water can make it more difficult for them to catch sight of their prey, which is forced to swim deeper, out of puffins' easy reach.

A member of the auk family, the puffin is a smart black-and-white bird with a large, colourful bill and orange feet. It looks very like the other auks. Bigger than the little auk of northern waters, but

considerably smaller than the guillemot or razorbill, the puffin is smaller than a town pigeon. Guillemots and razorbills are mostly found nearer the coast than puffins, which may fly as much as 1500km (930 miles) or more from land.

Nesting along clifftops

In spring, puffins flock to their island breeding grounds, forming noisy, crowded colonies along grassy clifftops, and excavating breeding burrows. Most puffin colonies are on islands out of reach of predatory mammals – rats in particular, are inclined to wreak havoc, taking eggs and young birds – although the puffin's main predators are gulls and skuas. Some colonies are formed on accessible islands, however, and just a few on mainland sites.

The puffin's bill is at its largest and most colourful during the breeding season. As a general rule, birds with the most spectacular bills have the best chance of attracting a mate and displacing rivals.

Only mature adults that will actually breed attend the colonies at first. These birds grow the broadest and brightest bills with the most grooves, and have the brightest eye ornaments, signalling their supremacy to rival birds and potential mates alike. Males are usually a little larger than females and have much bigger bills, at least within their own colony. Bill sizes vary from colony to colony. Puffins around Britain have distinctly smaller bills than those living farther north.

PUFFIN FACT FILE

This portly, upright black-and-white bird is popularly called the sea parrot because of its colourful bill. The puffin lives mostly far from land, but comes ashore to breed along grassy clifftops.

● NAMES
Common names: puffin, Atlantic puffin
Scientific name: *Fratercula arctica*

● HABITAT
Breeds on coastal cliffs and islands – otherwise lives far out at sea

● DISTRIBUTION
Breeding colonies on cliffs and offshore islands, mostly along western and northern coasts of Britain; after breeding, British puffins travel as far as Newfoundland and North Africa

● STATUS
Around 580,000 pairs breed in Britain and 21,300 in Ireland

● SIZE
Length 26–29cm (10½–11½in); weight 320–500g (11¼–1 ½oz); bill 3–4cm (1¼–1½in) long and a similar depth; wingspan 50–60cm (20–24in)

● KEY FEATURES
Black upperparts and white below; breeding adult has wide, bright blue, red and yellow bill and white face; in winter the face is smoky grey and the bill duller and narrower

● HABITS
Flies far out to sea, diving for fish; comes ashore to breed

● VOICE
A wide variety of grunting and groaning calls at the colony – often from below ground in breeding burrows; generally silent at sea

● FOOD
Small fish, especially sand eels, sprats, small herring and young fish of the cod family, such as whiting, haddock and rocklings; adults may also eat small amounts of invertebrates such as crustaceans and small shrimp

● BREEDING
Most birds arrive at the colony in late March or early April, lay eggs up to a few weeks later, leaving when the chicks fledge in late July to mid-August

● NEST
Up to 2m (6½ft) from the entrance to a burrow excavated in a grassy cliff edge or clifftop; old rabbit holes may be used; burrow often scattered with feathers, grass or other material brought in by adults but not used as nest lining

● EGGS
Single, big chalky white egg; incubated, mainly by female, for 36–45 days

● YOUNG
Single chick is fed on small fish by both parents; typically fledges in 36–40 days

During the breeding season, the almost triangular bill grows a prominent red and yellow horny covering.

The stocky, powerful body has the typical auk pattern of black upperparts and white face, breast and underparts.

Bright orange webbed feet are used as rudders underwater, for paddling and also for braking as the bird lands.

Distribution map key

▨ Present during spring and summer months

☐ Not present

Puffin courtship

These birds generally mate for life but separate for the winter. They meet once a year at the breeding site, where it is vital to re-establish the pair bond because both parents must work together to raise their chick.

When a puffin finds its mate, the pair greet each other by knocking their massive bills together alternately left and right as they shake their heads to and fro. This is known as 'billing'.

Sometimes one uses its bill to nuzzle or nibble the base of its partner's bill.

Should a mate fail to return, the survivor introduces itself to a potential new mate in the same way. Rivals may fight by locking bills.

Single chicks

Puffins breed just once each year. Although they sometimes attempt to copulate beside the burrow, or possibly even in it, puffins mostly mate on the sea directly below the colony. The female uses up much of her strength and condition in producing just a single egg. If chicks are lost when fish stocks are poor, there is no chance for pairs to produce any more young that year.

As a counterbalance to their low breeding rate, puffins have long lives. This ensures that they produce enough young to keep numbers from declining. Ringing has shown that many puffins live to 15 years of age, and some individuals reach almost 30 years.

Catching fish

Once the chick has hatched, the parents feed it fish. Puffins can catch many small fish – up to 12 and sometimes more – on

By carrying fish crossways in its bill, neatly impaled on the backward-pointing spines on the roof of its mouth, the puffin can catch a number of fish without having to swallow.

DID YOU KNOW?
Ringed British puffins have been found all over the north Atlantic, in the Mediterranean and off the North African coast. Many birds do not come to land at all in their first year. For the next year or two, they appear at colonies late in the breeding season, although not necessarily at the one where they hatched. Some young birds from St Kilda travel as far as Newfoundland, and several Scottish birds have been found in Greenland.

a single hunting expedition. The record is held jointly by a puffin arriving at a Scottish colony with 61 tiny sand eels and one rockling, and a Norwegian bird with more than 60 unidentified fish. Puffins carry the fish inside their bills crossways, neatly arranged head to tail. If a colony is doing well, birds return from the sea with at least half a dozen plump little fish each. If large numbers of birds return with only one slender fish each, the puffin colony is in trouble. Recent fishing by human beings for the

▶ Puffins generally form colonies along grassy clifftops where they can dig secure burrows. Some birds nest in natural nooks and crannies in cliffs and on boulder-strewn screes, while others take over rabbit holes.

▼ Colonies are crowded and, at prime sites, such as St Kilda, there may be a total of more than 140,000 pairs nesting on the grassy slopes during the breeding season.

PUFFIN CALENDAR

OCTOBER • FEBRUARY

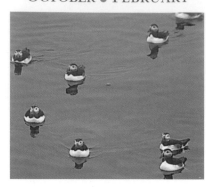

Puffins spend the winter far out at sea, mostly on their own but sometimes in very loose flocks. Their faces are grey and their bills are much duller and less noticeable than later in the year.

MARCH

The puffins' bills have grown their colourful, ridged covering, and their face feathers are changing to white. As the breeding season approaches, the birds fly back to their breeding colonies.

APRIL

Mated birds perform prolonged bouts of bowing and billing. These activities are a source of stimulation for neighbouring birds, and often trigger a frenzy of activity across the colony.

MAY

The female lays a single egg and spends most of her time incubating it. She remains alert, warning off non-breeding birds that enter looking for an unoccupied burrow.

JUNE • JULY

The chick is fed on small fish brought in by the adults, which have to avoid food-stealing gulls, skuas and jackdaws. In the week before the chick fledges, it eats less and loses weight.

AUGUST • SEPTEMBER

When it's ready to leave the nest, the chick makes its way to the shore in darkness, and flies off alone to live out at sea. Juvenile birds may not come ashore for a year or more.

puffin's staple food of sand eels has badly affected the puffin population in places such as Shetland.

Fish brought back by puffins are spied by other birds, including gulls, skuas, crows, ravens, jackdaws, Arctic terns and razorbills. These birds try to steal fish from the puffins before they can reach the burrows to feed their young. Agile skuas harry the puffins to induce them to drop their fish, then dive and seize the food. On landing, puffins dart down their holes as quickly as possible to avoid being attacked by great black-backed gulls or great skuas, both major predators. One reason for puffins nesting in colonies is that there is safety in numbers.

Half-grown chicks of some other members of the auk family are enticed off the nesting ledge and into the sea by their

Puffins choose remote places to nest not only to avoid rats, but to remain close to the sea. They select places where food, such as sand eels, is plentiful, so that they can provide for their growing chicks.

fathers, who then keep them company for many weeks. By contrast, puffin chicks remain in the burrow and are fed by their parents until they choose to leave. In some areas young puffins are drawn to congregate beside man-made structures. For example, when the lighthouse on Sule Skerry ran a generator, young puffins were attracted to the generator shed because its vibrations sounded like waves breaking on the shore.

Flight displays

The more chance there is of having their fish stolen, or of being preyed upon, the more likely puffins are to perform a spectacular wheeling flight. In a light wind, several hundred birds circle within a couple of metres of the ground. If winds are strong, they may fly in a figure-of-eight pattern. While individual birds probably circle a few times only, one circle display may last for a quarter of an hour or more.

In the evenings puffins often take off from their burrows, flying low and slowly. They hold their wings rather stiffly, the fluttering beats of their wing tips sounding above the burrows before the birds head out to sea. These are known as moth flights because the puffin's slow, fluttering flight is reminiscent of that of moths, and, for some unknown reason, puffins keep their legs crossed during them. Puffins engaged in moth flights appear to invite others to join them, sometimes circling the colony again to try to pick up more birds. Colour-ringing studies, whereby distinctively coloured lightweight plastic rings are fitted to the birds' legs, have shown that breeding pairs often fly together.

Threats to puffins

The Norse word for puffin is '*lund*', found in several place names, such as the island of Lundy in the Bristol Channel, which still has a small colony of puffins. For centuries, notably on remote islands such as St Kilda, humans ate puffins and used their feathers to stuff mattresses. Shooting puffins at sea for food and as fish bait is now illegal but was once widely practised. Today, humans compete with puffins for fish and use fishing nets in which diving

Like many seabirds, the puffin uses its outspread webbed feet as stabilisers to provide extra control during flight, and as 'air-brakes' when coming in to land.

puffins become entangled. Puffins are less vulnerable to oil pollution than the other auks because they live mainly out at sea and most oil spills happen close to shore.

The gradual warming of the sea may be a problem for puffins. They are essentially Arctic birds that have spread south to Britain, and are adapted to feeding in cold waters on small shoaling fish.

Puffin flight

This bird is not the most elegant of fliers, its chunky body and short wings giving it a whirring, laborious-looking style. Yet its sturdy, compact shape enables the puffin to fly in the harsh conditions that might leave other birds grounded.

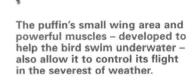

The puffin's small wing area and powerful muscles – developed to help the bird swim underwater – also allow it to control its flight in the severest of weather.

As it steps off the edge of the cliff, the gale-force winds blowing off the sea lift the bird into the air.

A stiff breeze at sea level often becomes a turbulent gale at the puffin's clifftop nesting site. As a prelude to taking off, the bird spreads its wings.

WILDLIFE WATCH

Where can I see puffins?

● The most accessible sites are on the mainland, such as Flamborough Head in Yorkshire, St Abbs Head in the Scottish Borders, and several coastal sites in Aberdeenshire. For large colonies, however, it is necessary to visit outlying islands.

● The Farne Islands have around 56,000 pairs, easily visited in summer from Seahouses on the Northumberland coast. Nearby Coquet Island has around 18,000 pairs.

● On the remote island group of St Kilda, off the west coast of Scotland, there are some 140,000 breeding pairs. Access is very difficult – visits must be arranged in organised groups through the National Trust for Scotland. Within easier reach, about 42,000 pairs nest on the Isle of May in the Firth of Forth.

The shelduck

On rivers and estuaries, shelducks in bright, new breeding plumage lay claim to nutrient-rich mudflats. Once paired, the birds seek out old rabbit burrows, often some distance away, where they can nest in safety.

In the early morning on estuaries all around the British Isles, as the sun rises and the tide falls, vast expanses of shiny mud are exposed. The landscape may look bleak, but the mudflats are brimming with food, attracting flocks of seabirds. Among the thousands of waders are the large shelducks.

Strictly speaking, shelducks are neither ducks nor geese, but belong to a small intermediate group called the Tadornini, which also includes the sheldgeese. They are different from other wildfowl in the way they nest and care for their young.

Although shelducks can appear black and white from a distance, closer inspection reveals a bottle-green head and neck, a band of chestnut across the breast and back and dark wing patches, contrasting with a blood-red bill and legs. These markings make the shelduck one of the most distinctive of all British waterfowl. The male is larger and brighter than the female and has a pronounced knob on his upper bill between his eyes.

Feeding habits

The shelduck has a very specialised diet. On British estuaries, its main food is *Hydrobia ulvae*, a tiny snail that lives in the mud and can occur in vast numbers, perhaps as many as 60,000 per square metre (5500 per sq ft). The shelduck feeds by using its broad, slightly up-turned bill to scoop up beakfuls of mud, snails and water, filtering out the snails via tiny serrations, called lamellae, at the sides of its bill.

Shelducks adopt different feeding techniques depending on the state of the tide. When the mud is soup-like and the prey is near the surface, they sweep their bills from side to side as they walk. A muddy estuary at low tide often displays patterns in the mud created by feeding shelducks. A continuous line shows where a bird has pushed its bill along as it filtered out the *Hydrobia*, and on either side are the prints of webbed feet. When the tide is rising or falling, however, shelducks upend to reach the muddy bottom and find snails that tend to emerge only when covered with water.

Despite its large size, the distinctively marked shelduck rises quite easily from the water, sometimes using a run-up to gain enough momentum for take off.

SHELDUCK FACT FILE

This goose-like bird is common around the coasts of Britain, on inland lakes and waterways, where it may be seen upending in shallow water or shovelling mud in search of food. The sexes are alike but the female has no knob at the base of the blood-red bill.

● **NAME**
Common name: shelduck
Scientific name: *Tadorna tadorna*

● **HABITAT**
Muddy and sandy coasts; some inland sites including lakes and sand and gravel workings

● **DISTRIBUTION**
All around coast of Britain and Ireland, except far north of Scotland and much of western Ireland; increasing numbers breed inland, especially in central and southern England

● **STATUS**
Almost 11,000 pairs in Britain plus about 1100 pairs in Ireland; also about 38,000 non-breeding individuals in Britain in summer and about 3900 in Ireland

● **SIZE**
Length 58–65cm (23–25½in); weight 926–1450g (2lb–3lb 4oz); wingspan 100–120cm (40–48in)

● **KEY FEATURES**
Adult has a mainly white body with dark green head and upper neck; conspicuous broad rufous breast and back band; black flight feathers, tail tip and belly stripe; blood-red bill and legs, male has red knob at base of bill; juvenile brownish grey and white with paler pinkish grey bill and legs and no breast or back band

● **HABITS**
Territorial at start of breeding season, gregarious at most other times; adults undertake moult migration, leaving young behind in crèches

● **VOICE**
Male usually silent or makes sweet-sounding whistles; female gives a lower, growling *'aaark, aaark'* call

● **FOOD**
Mainly invertebrates, especially tiny snails and molluscs, insects and crustaceans; inland worms and some vegetable matter

● **BREEDING**
Late April–May; moult migration July–November

● **NEST**
A shallow depression, lined with down feathers; sited in old rabbit burrow, hollow tree or some other hole, including in farm buildings, or even in dense vegetation

● **EGGS**
Clutch of 8–10, sometimes 12, smooth, rounded, creamy white eggs; several females may use single nest; hatch after 29–31 days

● **YOUNG**
Black-and-white chicks fledge in 45–50 days and join others to form large crèche of up to 100, overseen by a few adults

Having left the sanctuary of its nest, a fast-developing young shelduck searches for food. The chicks stay in contact with their siblings and parents for safety, returning to the adults when alarmed.

Distribution map key

■ Present all year round

□ Not present

Head and upper neck are dark green.

Wings are white with black flight feathers.

In males, the bright red bill has a prominent red knob at its base.

Conspicuous orange-chestnut breast band.

PROTECTED!

Unusually among wildfowl, the shelduck receives year-round protection under European law. There is no hunting season.

◄ In early spring, male shelducks seldom leave the side of their chosen mate. The head-back posture is often adopted during the breeding season as a prelude to the ritualised head-pumping display.

▲ If a man-made structure, such as a hay barn, becomes available, a shelduck is quite likely to take advantage of this warm, sheltered location to build its nest.

In recent years, shelducks have been seen inland increasingly often. They now regularly breed away from the coast, especially in England and parts of southern Scotland. This shift is probably due to a growing coastal population of shelducks that has filled most of the available habitat, forcing some birds to look for new territories inland. The expansion has been helped by birds using newly created reservoirs and flooded sand and gravel pits.

Territory defence
Spring is a good time to watch shelduck because the birds exhibit some interesting behaviour at this time of year. Pairs of adult birds begin to defend their feeding territories, performing several ritualised movements. Adults approach each other with a bowing action and the males enact a curious head-pumping display, during which the head appears to turn in a complete circle. Pairs also prospect for nesting sites at this time, and these may or may not be within the feeding territory. Some nests are as much as two miles away.

Shelducks nest in holes of various kinds, including gaps under buildings, spaces between straw bales and holes in trees, sometimes several feet off the ground. However, most often these birds will adopt an abandoned rabbit burrow, especially where sand dunes fringe the coast. The nest may be sited as much as 3m (10ft) down the tunnel. Although shelduck pairs will defend their feeding territories from trespassers, nesting females are very tolerant of each other. Indeed, two or three females may even share different chambers in the same rabbit burrow.

The nest is made of a small amount of grass or straw, which is gathered from the vicinity of the nest, and lined with copious amounts of down that the female plucks from her own breast. In this insulated underground nest, the duck lays a clutch of up to 12 round, creamy white eggs, usually in early May.

Attracting a mate

Most female shelducks wait until they are about two years old to find a mate, and the bond that is formed will usually last for life. The female uses 'incitement behaviour' to attract the attention of a male. She may even direct her posturing at several males, encouraging them to compete for her favours.

The male remains aloof, but his response to her display may decide whether she chooses him or not.

At first, the female walks parallel to a chosen male, holding her head low and seeming to point with her bill, often at a rival male.

SHELDUCK CALENDAR

JANUARY • FEBRUARY

Adult pairs often stay together within the winter flocks that form where feeding is good. Flocks begin to break up as pairs disperse to their breeding grounds on larger estuaries.

MARCH • APRIL

The male defends the pair's feeding territory while they search for a nesting area, which may be several miles away. The first creamy white eggs are laid in late April.

MAY • JUNE

The female incubates the eggs for about a month, joining her mate only to feed. The parents lead the recently hatched young to a nursery area, and defend them vigorously.

JULY • AUGUST

Some adults remain with their young until they fledge about two months later, but most fly off to moult, leaving their offspring in a crèche watched over by a few 'aunties'.

SEPTEMBER • OCTOBER

Most adults gather on moulting grounds in the Heligoland Bight tidal estuaries off the north German coast. They lose their flight feathers and become flightless for four weeks or so.

NOVEMBER • DECEMBER

When the adults return, their young have already dispersed in the local area. Large flocks form where food is plentiful, and birds move from estuary to estuary.

Raising his body on straight legs, the male gives chase. He may also begin a rotary pumping movement of his head, intended to intimidate any rivals.

The female makes a scooping motion with her head and neck to point her bill skywards. Once a bond is established, the male may attack any rival males that are still lingering around his new mate.

Keeping close to the male, the female suddenly cuts across his path, raising her head as she does so.

Sifting out food

Shelducks have voracious appetites and favour tidal mudflats that contain large quantities of tiny snails. The birds adapt their feeding technique to the state of the tide, dabbling in deeper water or scything the bill through liquid mud on the shore.

The shelduck sweeps its bill through the watery mud to bring food items to the surface from where they can be scooped up.

Juvenile shelducks differ from the adults in being mainly white with grey-brown upperparts. They seem to know instinctively how to move their bills through the water in search of food, which is vital since they must feed themselves from the moment they hatch.

Some nests have been found to contain a much larger than usual number of eggs – up to 32 in one case. These large clutches are the result of egg-dumping, when several females lay their eggs in a single nest. The egg-dumpers are usually young females that lack breeding experience.

Eggs are laid at a rate of one per day, but the female does not begin to incubate them until the clutch is complete. After four weeks of incubation, all the eggs will hatch more or less simultaneously. The female incubates alone – hissing furiously at any intruders – but the male is never far away.

The young leave the nest soon after they hatch. The adults abandon their feeding territory and one or both of them leads the new family to a nursery area.

The black-and-white ducklings are able to feed themselves straight away and can dive expertly if threatened. At this time, the parents will aggressively defend their youngsters from predators and other shelducks, and will even attack the young of other birds. It seems that shelducks are hostile towards other chicks that attempt to join their family group. However, if the trespassing young are the same size as their own chicks, the parents can sometimes become confused and accidentally attack their own offspring.

The young are fully independent after 45 to 50 days, but from 14 days they may be effectively independent of their parents. Then they tend to join up in the nursery, the mixed broods forming 'crèches' of up to 100 ducklings. The young of various ages gradually mix together, and the older, larger ducklings can sometimes be seen brooding the smaller ones. By July, flotillas of young shelducks of various ages may be seen around the coasts. These crèches are accompanied for a time by a few adults, known as 'aunties'. They may be breeding birds or the inexperienced females that dumped their eggs in another shelduck's nest. The latter have no way of knowing whether any of the ducklings in the crèche are their own, therefore their presence in the nursery ground may be pure coincidence. Eventually, even the aunties will leave the ducklings in order to moult.

Moulting feathers

Some families will stay together for up to nine weeks until the young are able to fly, but this is exceptional. Most family groups start to break down after two to three weeks, as the adult birds feel the overriding urge to undertake a moult migration. This is a journey to a traditional place where the birds can safely moult their flight feathers and grow new ones, a trip that is not to be confused with any seasonal migrations. For example, some species of geese fly north to their moulting grounds before heading south on their true migration in autumn.

Few shelducks wait for their young to become independent before setting out for their moulting grounds. In July, most breeding adults and immature birds will depart for the Heligoland Bight in Germany, where an estimated 200,000 or more shelducks have often been seen off the Elbe estuary. Some shelducks do not

Shelducks are vigilant parents and keep a constant eye on their troop of youngsters. The soft mud of the estuary provides some security from ground predators, such as foxes, but gulls remain a threat.

go abroad to moult, several thousand of them congregating in a few large estuaries in Britain, notably Bridgwater Bay off the Somerset coast. There are additional flocks in the Wash in East Anglia and the Firth of Forth in Scotland.

Shelducks form large groups as they prepare to moult their flight feathers. It seems that even at this time some breeding pairs will remain together, and they can be distinguished within the flock. Each member of the pair will use a special head-up salute to indicate that they intend to take flight. All ducks are vulnerable when moulting because, unlike most other birds, they lose all their flight feathers at once and become flightless until new ones grow. For shelducks, this period may be as long as 31 days.

Leisurely journey

By October, new flight feathers have grown and the shelducks return to their feeding and breeding areas. The journey is not necessarily direct, and shelducks may visit a succession of estuaries before finally reaching their breeding grounds. During the winter, flocks build up where food is plentiful, and it may not be until early spring that feeding territories are established once more.

While the adults are on the moult migration, the juveniles disperse widely from the nesting area. Young from the same brood may travel in different directions and some British birds even reach mainland Europe.

Shelducks are gregarious birds, except when breeding, and large numbers build up on wintering grounds. The birds are usually scattered when feeding, but may gather in dense flocks where food is concentrated.

For birds that spend much of their time in salty water, feather care is very important. The shelduck must spend a large amount of time washing and preening to keep its plumage in good condition.

Shelducks that live in areas of salt and brackish water can find food throughout most winters. Only when ice and snow freeze the ground is there high mortality. If both members of a pair survive, the same birds are likely to mate and produce a new family the following spring.

At a time when so many birds are threatened by environmental changes, the shelduck appears to be a winner. In fact, Britain has the largest population of shelducks in north-west Europe. Until recently, the ecological importance of estuaries and mudflats was not realised but now these are largely protected. However, with climate changes and sea levels rising, the coastline may change, and the fate of the shelduck remains uncertain.

WILDLIFE WATCH

Where can I see shelducks?

● The shelduck is a conspicuous bird and fairly easy to watch, especially in spring. Visit estuaries such as the Wash in East Anglia, Morecambe Bay in Lancashire, the Gower Peninsula in south Wales and the Firth of Forth in Scotland. Wander along the tide line, especially where there are mudflats and salt marshes, to see the birds feeding.

● Listen out for the shelduck's calls, especially those of the females. Noise travels well across mudflats and the characteristic growling call often reveals the presence of females. They frequently feed in a creek or channel out of sight of the shore.

● RSPB coastal reserves often have shelducks, including Minsmere in Suffolk, Snettisham in Norfolk, Elmley in Kent, Langstone Harbour in Hampshire, Blacktoft Sands in East Riding of Yorkshire, Conwy in north Wales and Mersehead, Dumfries and Galloway. For details, telephone 01767 680551 or visit www.rspb.org

● Some inland reservoirs, such as Rutland Water near Oakham and Grafham Water near Huntingdon, have breeding populations of shelducks.

The common lobster

Concealed in its rocky lair below low-tide level, the common lobster lurks unseen, ready to protect itself with its fearsome claws, and detecting any sign of danger with its sensitive red antennae.

One of the common lobster's pincers is usually larger than the other, and is used for crushing. The smaller claw is a sharper-edged cutting tool.

Along with crabs, prawns and crayfish, the common lobster is a crustacean, characterised by its extremely hard outer shell. It is the largest and strongest of all British crustaceans and can live as long as 50 years. The biggest recorded British individual was landed at Cornwall in 1931, weighing a massive 9.3kg (20lb 8oz).

Reclusive giant

For all its size, the lobster lives a secluded life by day, lodged in a crevice in the rock with only its sensitive antennae and well-armoured pincers projecting. It cannot easily be prised out because these formidable claws act as an effective deterrent, while its other limbs and tail grip the walls of its lair.

The lobster will usually leave its home at night to roam the seabed in search of food. This comprises a variety of shellfish and other bottom-living creatures. The lobster also scavenges on the remains of dead animals that have fallen to the seabed and it will take small fish and squid if they come close enough to catch.

The lobster uses strong abdominal muscles to power its swimming limbs for forward movement, and the rapid flexing of its tail enables it to reverse quickly away from potential danger. As well as crushing shellfish, the lobster uses its impressive claws – known as chelae – to fight other lobsters that may inadvertently wander into its territory. The claws are also used in defence – the lobster's pincers have a strong grip and can inflict painful damage to a human finger.

In common with many animals, lobsters will not readily pass up available food that they come across while foraging. If they collect too much for their immediate needs, they will bury the excess in the sediment near their lair, bulldozing sand over the cache and using their legs and mouthparts to rearrange the pile, effectively disguising it.

LOBSTER RELATIVES

A close relative of the common lobster is the Norway lobster (*Nephrops norvegicus*), also known as the Dublin Bay prawn. Smaller than the common lobster, it has elegant pincers as long as its body. It lives in a burrow in the soft seabed around the British Isles, emerging only to forage. Its flesh, known by the Italian name *'scampi'*, is considered a delicacy in Britain.

Another fairly close relative is the common crawfish (*Palinurus elephas*), or spiny lobster, which is found only in waters off western Britain and Ireland. The crawfish is usually reddish brown, and lacks the huge pincers of its more colourful relatives. These crustaceans are also caught by commercial fishermen and many are exported as *'langouste'*.

COMMON LOBSTER FACT FILE

The slow-growing common lobster takes many years to mature. Periodically, its hard outer shell splits across the back and the lobster pulls itself out. It may eat the discarded shell to replace lost calcium.

● **NAMES**
Common names: common lobster, European lobster
Scientific name: *Homarus gammarus*

● **HABITAT**
Holes, crevices and tunnels excavated in soft sediment on rocky seabed from the lower shore to a depth of about 60m (200ft); emerges to feed on seabed at night

● **DISTRIBUTION**
All around British coasts but much more common in the west; rare in waters with a sandy seabed

● **STATUS**
Declining

● **SIZE**
Length up to around 75cm (30in), but rarely more than 30cm (12in); weight up to about 7kg (15lb 8oz); size depends on amount of food available

● **KEY FEATURES**
Two large but unequal pincers; long bright red antennae; deep blue colour with yellowish to rust-coloured fringes to the body. Has a potential life span of 15–50 years, but most are caught long before reaching old age

● **HABITS**
Nocturnal, retreats to lair among rocks and seaweed during day

● **FOOD**
Carnivorous scavenger and hunter; eats molluscs, smaller crustaceans (including other lobsters) and other invertebrates

● **BREEDING**
Usually mates in late summer or early autumn; female carries thousands of eggs, storing sperm to fertilise them the following spring

● **YOUNG**
Resemble adults

Ever alert, the lobster uses its very long, bright red antennae to test the water constantly for chemicals and signs of movement.

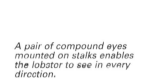

Distribution map key

■ Present all year round

□ Not present

A pair of compound eyes mounted on stalks enables the lobster to see in every direction.

Each joint allows movement in one direction only.

Many-jointed abdomen allows flexible movement.

Pincers at the end of the enormous claws have sharp serrations, which give the lobster a secure grip.

Thin, spindly legs are used for scuttling along the seabed.

PROTECTED!

It is illegal to take lobsters less than 87mm (3½in) in length, excluding claws and tail, or females that are carrying eggs – a condition known as 'in berry'.

Highly territorial, an adult lobster is ever ready to use its giant claws to inflict serious damage, or even kill, a rival lobster.

paddle-like swimming organs called 'swimmerets' arise from the abdomen, and finally, at the end of the body, there is the fan-like tail.

Armour plating

The lobster's tough exoskeleton acts as armour to protect the soft internal organs, but the rigidity of the body and limbs creates problems for the lobster because it loses some flexibility. Each leg-joint is a hinge that bends in one direction only. In order to achieve all-round movement, every leg has to have several sections that bend in different planes, like the arm of an angle-poise lamp.

The other drawback of carrying around a strong, protective carapace is that continuous growth is constrained. Lobsters grow by undertaking a series of moults whereby the hard outer shell is shed, revealing a softer shell that is able to stretch as the lobster puffs up its body. After a while the new shell hardens, although the lobster is very vulnerable during this process. It makes an easy meal for predators, which include other lobsters.

All parts of the lobster's exterior, even the eyes – which are covered by a chalky skeleton – must be discarded, or cast, to allow growth. The first and last regions of the gut are lined with a thin skeleton, and this too must be shed with the rest. Within the first section of the gut, a grinding apparatus, called the gastric mill, is composed of chalky plates that crush the food before it enters the mid-gut.

Mouthparts on the head are used to shred food and transfer the particles into the mouth. The lobster's food then passes through three stomachs.

specialised functions, such as feeding, walking and swimming. This adaptation can be seen in the lobster today. The two front segments each bear a pair of antennae, behind which, around the mouth, six pairs of appendages act like cutlery for feeding. These are followed by the two gigantic pincers for feeding and fighting, and four pairs of legs that are used for locomotion. Five pairs of

Crustaceans, including lobsters, belong to a group known as arthropods. This group, which includes insects and spiders, comprises creatures with segmented, jointed limbs – 'arthro' means jointed and 'poda' means legs. The earliest arthropods, which lived around 550 million years ago, possessed segmented bodies with a pair of identical appendages arising from each segment. Over time, these uniform limbs took on different forms, allowing them to perform

LOBSTER'S EYE VIEW

Lobsters have compound eyes that are held forward on stalks. At the back of the eyes there are many conical tubes, each an individual light-sensitive organ, focusing on an optic nerve at its base. At the top of each tube is a lens overlaid by a circle of transparent cuticle. The sight that results from so many tubes is blurred, because together they form a mosaic picture, made up of many over-lapping images. However, the eyes are efficient at detecting movement, and this is adequate for the lobster's way of life.

The lobster's body is equipped with an impressive array of sense organs, including many hairs that cover the body and respond to touch and chemical stimuli. The lobster has two sorts of antennae. The first pair is sensitive to chemicals and the second to vibrations.

The eyes of lobsters and crawfish are made up of hundreds of light-sensitive tubes which, between them, scan the whole surrounding area. They work well in poor light, but do not focus such detailed images as human eyes do.

Tiny balance organs called statocysts are located at the base of the antennae to help the lobster maintain its posture. The statocysts consist of small capsules containing tiny fragments of chalk lying in a surrounding fluid. If the body tilts, the particles move relative to the capsule walls and excite little sensory hairs to inform the animal of the angle of its body.

The common lobster is naturally a beautiful dark blue colour due to a pigment called astaxanthin in its shell.

These plates also lose their hard skeletal surface during the moult. One advantage of moulting is that it periodically rids the carapace of unwanted barnacles and other encrusting hitch-hikers.

A surprising feature of the armoured limbs is that they can be sacrificed to a predator by breaking across a built-in weak point. Here, special muscles snap off the limb and close over the wound. The predator departs with its booty and the lobster's limb regenerates. Soft tissues build up at the wound and at each moult they grow outwards a little bit more until the limb is back to its normal size.

Lobster reproduction

Most lobsters start breeding after their fifth year, and then reproduce annually. The female must mate during a moult and she secretes a special hormone to prevent the male from eating her. Mating occurs in late summer or early autumn,

when the male transfers a number of spermatophores (parcels of sperm) to the female using the first two of his abdominal swimming limbs. The female holds several thousand eggs in a mucous net around her limbs and the following spring she moves inshore to fertilise them by releasing the stored sperm.

Nine months after mating, the eggs hatch into tiny lobsters a millimetre or so long. They are at their most vulnerable at this stage. For the next 12 days they swim in the plankton, growing rapidly and undergoing several moults. They then sink to the seabed and burrow into the sediment. At about 2cm (⅜in) long they look like miniature adults. When they are about 20cm (8in) long they emerge to find a suitable crevice in which to hide. Here they will spend their adult lives.

Conservation issues

Over the past few decades lobsters have been under increasing pressure from pollution and global warming as well as

overfishing. Removal rates have been estimated at up to 70 per cent. One way of conserving populations is to ban fishing in a specific area. In 2003 an area to the east of Lundy Island, off the Devon coast, was designated a No-Take Zone, whereby the removal of any living creature, including lobsters, was prohibited by law. In July 2005, after just two years, there were three times more lobsters of landable size in the No-Take Zone compared to fished areas.

Another way to help, which is employed by lobster hatcheries, is to raise lobsters from eggs. In the wild just five in 1000 baby lobsters reach adulthood. By releasing young lobsters when they are past the most vulnerable stage in their life cycle, survival rates are greatly enhanced.

Short, weak legs are used for balance and forward movement rather than support. On the inside of the legs short bristles called 'hedgehog hairs' continually 'taste' the water for signs of food.

The periwinkle

Found on rocky shores, the most abundant sea snail in Britain is the periwinkle. It clusters in crevices along the upper and middle shore zones, although some prefer the bottom of rock pools.

Periwinkles are gastropods – a type of mollusc that has a soft body, a single coiled shell and sucker-like foot, and eyes and feelers on a head. The garden snail is also a gastropod, as is the limpet.

Found on many shores around Britain, different periwinkles occupy distinct levels of the shore. While some are easy to name, others are only now being identified using DNA fingerprinting techniques to discover to which family they belong. Periwinkles are so numerous that the upper shore is sometimes referred to as the 'littorine zone', after the periwinkle's scientific name *Littorina.*

Some periwinkles prefer to live above the high-water mark, along parts of the shore that are possibly reached by the splash from waves at high tide. Others live along the middle shore where they are exposed for just a short time by the receding tide. Periwinkles are also plentiful in rock pools, particularly those which are covered with rich organic matter on which to feed.

Different sizes

The largest periwinkle is, not surprisingly, the one most often eaten by human beings. The edible, or common, periwinkle (*Littorina littorea*) is up to 3cm (1¼in) high and dark greyish brown or black, or occasionally reddish, in colour. It is marked with faint spiral striations around the whorls of its shell, which has a white edge to the opening. Almost as big is the black-lined periwinkle (*Littorina nigrolineata*), which has an almost globular shell that is whitish, yellow or orange, or a deep orange marked with dark brown.

Next in size is the rough periwinkle (*Littorina saxatilis*). These are mostly under 1.5cm (⅝in) high, with ridges and grooves around their shells. The flat periwinkles (*Littorina obtusata* and *Littorina mariae*) are about 1cm (½in) high

▶ Sheltered crevices are favoured by periwinkles living on exposed rocky shores where the rocks are regularly pounded by the sea. In some places there are so many individuals crammed into a crevice that they pile up three or four deep.

▲ Periwinkles discovered on a single beach can exhibit a wide range of colour variation. This means that at least a proportion of the population will be camouflaged against the underwater surfaces of the shoreline, which also vary in colour.

Flat periwinkles resemble the air bladders of the two seaweeds on which they feed. This camouflage disguises them from numerous predators, including various shore birds.

and can be of almost any colour, depending on parentage and diet. Finally, there are the small periwinkles, which are blue-black in colour and rarely more than 0.5cm (¼in) high.

Scraping up food

Like most other sea snails, periwinkles feed by rasping at hard surfaces with a file-like tongue – the radula. This is pushed out of the mouth and scraped over the rock to remove any food that may be present. The small periwinkle's favourite foods are tiny algae and lichens but the other species feed mainly on larger seaweeds. The edible periwinkle, for instance, eats sea-lettuce and gut weed, while flat and rough periwinkles graze on egg wrack and bladder wrack.

◄ Flat periwinkles lay their eggs in jelly that adheres to seaweed. The jelly stops the developing young from drying out when the weed is exposed to sun.

► In common with other snails, periwinkles move using a muscular foot that glides along on a trail of slime. The foot clamps on to rocks and seaweeds to stop the animal being washed away

Breeding methods

For all periwinkles, the breeding process begins with the male planting sperm within the female's body during mating. Thereafter, different periwinkles reproduce by a variety of means, depending on the amount of time they spend out of water.

The periwinkles highest on the shore set free egg capsules fortnightly on spring tides, so that the young have a good chance of being washed into the sea. The young spend a few weeks in the plankton, growing a shell and an adhesive foot. Then they climb to a position as high on the shore as that occupied by their parents.

The rough periwinkle and its close relative *Littorina neglecta* are often found on the west coasts of Britain alongside the small periwinkle high on the shore, but also lower down than the high-tide mark. Their young do not have a stage of growing in the plankton. These periwinkles brood their young throughout the year, carrying 50 to 100 embryos, all at different stages of development. The young are released directly on to the shore as they mature into miniature adults. The black-lined periwinkle lays egg masses in pink jelly all through the year. This method is also adopted by the flat periwinkles.

Different periwinkles have evolved around Britain's shores, probably over the past few million years. They have exploited a variety of food sources and adopted strategic means of reproducing so that they do not directly compete with each other. In this way, new types of periwinkles have evolved. Today, the rough periwinkle is continuing to develop into separate species. Different members of this family are already unable to interbreed. As these distinct groups reproduce, there is a gradual increase in their unique characteristics.

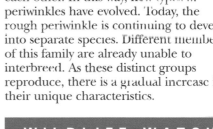

The tracks left on the bottom of rock pools are often the only clue to the activities of resident periwinkles. These animals may appear to be sedentary but they do travel short distances.

Coral

In shallow water, true corals attach themselves to rocks and harbour walls, waving their often translucent stinging tentacles in search of tiny animals to trap and eat.

The most abundant of the few true corals that live around Britain's coasts is the Devonshire cup coral, which is most likely to be seen at the bottom of rock pools in low water. Although often said to be a rarity, the Devonshire cup coral can be quite numerous where conditions are favourable on the southern and western coasts of Britain and Ireland. Where currents swirl around nooks and overhangs in shallow water, cup corals can be dotted about over rocks and jetties, even between tide marks.

If spotted before it is disturbed, a cup coral resembles a tiny sea anemone – it belongs to the same order – but when its soft tissues are retracted, all that remains to be seen is a little chalky skeleton, called the calyx, that looks like a stud from a football boot. The coral's ability to secrete a chalky skeleton from its base distinguishes it from other related creatures.

Coral has a bag-like body with a single mouth-like opening at the top. Through this opening it takes in food, ejects undigested morsels and excretes waste. The coral feeds and protects itself using a ring of tentacles around the top of its 'mouth'. These are heavily charged with stinging cells to catch food and deter predators, such as fish and crabs.

Rarer cup corals

Two other cup corals, seen far less often than Devonshire cup coral, are the scarlet-and-gold star coral and the sunset cup coral. These are such an attractive part of Britain's coastal wildlife that a study is under way to determine their numbers and survival rate.

In some places it is thought that the scarlet-and-gold star coral is being usurped by the Devonshire cup coral, possibly as a result of changing water quality. However, it is not certain whether this trend might lead to one coral totally

Although it looks similar to a sea anemone, the Devonshire cup coral differs in having a chalky skeleton. If it is disturbed, the animal withdraws into this protective case.

replacing the other. It seems that both the scarlet-and-gold star coral and the sunset cup coral favour fairly sheltered spots, such as crevices or overhangs, whereas the Devonshire cup coral also ventures on to more open sites, especially below low tide.

A recent survey suggests that star coral numbers around Lundy Island in the Bristol Channel – a marine nature reserve – have halved in the past 20 years. While this indicates a potential problem for the survival of star coral, some very small individuals were last seen in this monitored area about 30 years ago, demonstrating that star coral may have a life span of more than 30 years.

Cup corals provide an interesting example of organisms living together for their mutual benefit. Barnacles called

◄ Sunset cup coral lives off the coasts of Devon and Cornwall. It favours rocky overhangs to which it attaches its tapering skeleton. Each animal can have 90 or more tentacles.

► Although Devonshire cup coral – unlike many true corals – is essentially a solitary animal, several individuals may be found close to one another in suitable settings. As its name suggests, this coral is often found in Britain on the coasts of Devon and Cornwall.

Megatrema settle on the sides of the coral's skeletal calyx, with sometimes as many as five clinging to a single individual. The barnacles produce typical barnacle shells, from the top of which their feathery feeding legs rake the water for plankton. The barnacle's sides are enveloped by the coral's soft tissue, leaving the hole open at the top. This wrap appears to be necessary for the survival of the barnacle since, if the host's tissues are withdrawn, the barnacle dies.

The life stages of cup corals are similar to those of sea anemones, although little detail is known. The eggs and sperm are shed from separate sexes and the eggs are fertilised in open sea during the spring. The fertilised egg develops into a rather featureless larva called a planula, which is little more than a bundle of cells, with no gut, tentacles or other organs. Like most larvae of sedentary adults, the planula is able to test the sea bed before it settles to make sure that it is a suitable place for an adult cup coral to

live. Then it attaches itself to rock or wall by means of an adhesive disc before secreting its chalky skeleton to anchor it in place.

Deep sea coral
In deeper waters, beyond the reach of sunlight, lives a fascinating coral, *Lophelia*, that is not unlike tropical staghorn coral in appearance. This is the most plentiful of Britain's deep-sea corals, and it can be found in regions with strong currents off the western and northern coasts. Here it multiplies to produce vast coral beds sometimes many miles in length and up to 30m (100ft) deep. These are a haven for other creatures, and particularly for their young, which are as yet unable to fend for themselves on the open sea bed.

Chilly waters
However, corals do not generally flourish in temperate seas to the extent that they do in clear, tropical waters. Sea temperatures around Britain never exceed about 20°C (68°F), and most corals need an average of above 25°C (77°F) to build the chalky 'cities' that form the fringing reefs, barrier reefs and atolls of the tropics.

In tropical coral reefs, the huge skeletal mass that is formed – for example, the Great Barrier Reef off the north-eastern coast of Australia is 2300km (1425 miles) long and visible from space – is made possible by single-celled algae that live in

an interdependent relationship with the coral. In return for being sheltered by the coral, the algae give their host some of the food they are able to manufacture. This augments the food the coral catches with its tentacles. The algae also help the coral to extract calcium carbonate from the sea to build a skeleton. Strong sunlight, high temperatures and clear waters are needed for this process. In the cooler waters of the north-east Atlantic, Britain's corals are not supported by tiny algae and are therefore much slower to build their skeletons.

▲ Using 50 translucent, knobbed tentacles, the Devonshire cup coral sweeps the surrounding water, searching for tiny animals to paralyse and draw into its mouth.

► Misleadingly named, the ross coral – or rose coral – is actually from a different group of animals known as bryozoans. These form encrusting and self-supporting colonies on rock faces, with individual animals waving delicate feeding tentacles from myriad tiny pores.

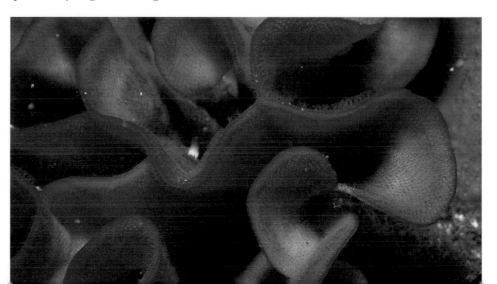

Sea urchins

The spiky sea urchins that live in British coastal waters are as attractive and colourful as any tropical species. On the sea bed, they move slowly on extended tube feet, seeking the security of forests of kelp when the tide recedes.

Spring and early summer is when sea urchins are at their most active. In common with many marine animals around the British coastline, urchins spawn then to take advantage of the yearly bloom of plankton on which their young will feed.

Along with starfish, sea cucumbers, brittlestars and featherstars, sea urchins belong to a group of spiny-skinned marine animals called the echinoderms. These animals are an important part of the coastal ecosystem and in some places make up a staggering 90 per cent of animals present. The echinoderms are characterised by a regular pattern of five rays on their skeleton and the presence of tube feet. In the sea urchin's case, the tube feet occur on five bands radiating around the almost spherical body, protruding through holes in its calcareous internal skeleton. Tube feet on the underside adhere to rocks by suction and mucus so that the sea urchin can move around. Tube feet elsewhere on the body are held taut to absorb oxygen from the surrounding water.

In British waters, some sea urchins live around all coasts, although some species no longer occur in the south-eastern region of the Channel. They feed on kelp and algae, as well as small sea creatures, and their constant grazing helps to keep kelp forests in check. When urchins have been experimentally excluded from kelp beds, or have disappeared because of disease or pollution, the kelp has grown too thickly for an understorey of smaller weeds to survive. In turn this has excluded animals that normally exist around such weeds. So the sea urchin is vital in maintaining the natural state of offshore reefs.

Conversely, population explosions of sea urchins can have a devastating effect on kelp forests, stripping large areas and leaving a barren 'urchin desert'. The reasons for such population explosions are not fully understood but could be the result of a local decline in natural predators, such as lobsters and crabs.

TEST CASE

The almost spherical internal skeleton of a sea urchin is called a 'test'. It comprises several bony plates, called ossicles, fused together in a kind of three-dimensional jigsaw. Looking at an empty test, it is easy to see the five-fold symmetry that typifies all echinoderms. Imagine taking a starfish by each of its arms and bending them upwards to join at the top – this is the basic design of the sea urchin.

The outer edge of an empty test may have rows of rounded white nodules. These are called tubercles and they held the urchin's spines. Rows of tiny paired holes show where the urchin's tube feet protruded from the shell.

The various species of sea urchin have different coloured tests. Cleaned up empty tests found on the beach make an attractive collection.

With hundreds of tiny tube feet acting in concert, sea urchins are capable of climbing up vertical rocks and kelp stems. The suction of their feet holds them firm during the roughest of storms.

COMMON SEA URCHIN FACT FILE

The scientific name Echinus *comes from the Greek word for 'hedgehog' and aptly describes the sea urchin's appearance. The attractive reddish violet test is a popular souvenir, so much so that overexploitation is a threat to the species in some areas.*

● NAMES
Common names: common sea urchin, edible sea urchin
Scientific name: *Echinus esculentus*

● HABITAT
Rocky shores with plenty of seaweed for grazing, usually below the low-water mark to 40m (130ft) deep

● DISTRIBUTION
All around the British Isles, especially in Scotland; absent from coasts around the south-east of England

● STATUS
Common and often abundant

● SIZE
Test up to 18cm (7in) in diameter

● KEY FEATURES
Generally pale rose-red colour

● HABITS
Mainly nocturnal

● FOOD
Seaweeds and tiny animals such as sea mats and sea firs

● BREEDING
In spring females release eggs into water with pheromones to induce nearby males to spawn

● YOUNG
Larvae float in plankton for several weeks before settling

Although it is most commonly a pale rose-red colour, the common sea urchin can be bluish green, purple or a very pale pink, almost white.

SHORE URCHIN FACT FILE

Like many other species of sea urchin, the shore urchin often drapes itself with camouflaging seaweed, shell fragments and even remnants of plastic. This is often enough to fool the fish and seals that regularly prey upon sea urchins.

● NAMES
Common names: shore urchin, green urchin, sea loch urchin
Scientific name: *Psammechinus miliaris*

● HABITAT
Rocky shores, never far above low-water mark down to a depth of 100m (330ft)

● DISTRIBUTION
Around most of the British Isles

● STATUS
Generally common on all coasts

● SIZE
Test up to 5cm (2in) in diameter

● KEY FEATURES
Test usually green, with greyish purple segments; spines greenish, tipped with violet; may appear pale brown to almost black

● HABITS
Mainly nocturnal

● FOOD
Barnacle larvae, young molluscs and other small animals as well as seaweeds

● BREEDING
Spawns in late spring–early summer

● YOUNG
Larvae live in plankton for several weeks; tiny urchins often found on strands of kelp

The strong, mobile spines of the shore urchin are purple-tipped, covering a globe-shaped skeleton.

ROCK URCHIN FACT FILE

Although the names suggest otherwise, it is mainly the rock urchin that is eaten as a delicacy, rather than the larger common, or edible, sea urchin. The edible part of the urchin is the gonad or roe inside the test.

● NAMES
Common names: rock urchin, purple urchin
Scientific name: *Paracentrotus lividus*

● HABITAT
Rocky shores, rarely above low-water mark and to a depth of about 30m (100ft)

● DISTRIBUTION
Mainly western Ireland

● STATUS
Can be abundant in parts of its limited range

● SIZE
Test up to 7cm (2¾in) in diameter

● KEY FEATURES
Variable in colour from dark violet to olive green, dark brown or almost black

● HABITS
Often burrows into rocks to hide

● FOOD
Feeds on seaweed fragments and spores carried into its burrow by the tide

● BREEDING
In spring females release eggs and pheromones in the water; males release sperm

● YOUNG
Larvae float in plankton for several weeks before turning into miniature adults and settling on rocky outcrops

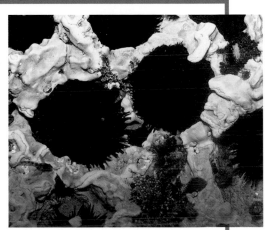

Rock urchins excavate their own burrows in the rock. As the urchin grows, it may become wedged in the space and never be able to leave.

Sea urchins scrape away at algae using a unique apparatus at the base of their body referred to as 'Aristotle's lantern'. This is named after the Greek philosopher, who was the first to describe the sea urchin in scientific terms. The lantern-shaped arrangement of muscles and ligaments manipulates five teeth in all directions to scrape weed off rock, masticate it and pass it into the gut.

Poisonous prickles

Perhaps the most notable feature of sea urchins is the spines. In British sea urchins, the spines are rarely longer than about 2cm (¾in), but in some tropical species, such as the hatpin urchin, they can be up to 23cm (9in) long, while those of the slate-pencil urchin are thick, with bands of colour. All urchin spines are covered with skin and secrete a poisonous mucus.

Hidden among the main spines, almost invisible to the naked eye, are tiny secret weapons called pedicellariae. Some are like three-jawed forceps, and the urchin uses these to keep its outer surface clear of any pests or debris. Like a street-cleaner picking up waste-paper with long-handled pincers, the pedicellariae grasp hold of the offending items and toss them away. The pedicellariae also grasp hold of food particles. Some pedicellariae carry poison

glands that are an effective defence against predators. Although the pedicellariae on British urchins are harmless to humans, the poison glands of some Indo-Pacific sea urchins have a serious effect on anybody handling them. It is said that an extract of just a few of these structures is sufficient to kill a person. Once used, a glandular pedicellaria is torn off and the urchin regenerates a new one.

Breeding cycle

Female common sea urchins mature in around two years, when they reach a diameter of about 2cm (¾in). In spring

Unlike the rotund common sea urchin, the shore urchin is decidedly flattened from top to bottom. This enables it to creep into the narrow spaces between boulders and rocks.

they release more than a million eggs in a fluid containing hormones that stimulate the males to spawn too, fertilising the eggs in the water. Populations of sea urchins synchronise their spawning, although zoologists are not certain how this is done.

The tiny larvae move up near the water's surface and grow long ciliated, or hairy, arms that they use to capture the minute plankton on which they feed. After four to eight weeks of feeding on the plankton, a cluster of cells in the lower left-hand side of the body starts to form the beginnings of a tiny urchin body, called a 'rudiment'. As the rudiment develops, adult features, such as tube feet, begin to appear, while larval structures, including the arms and even the larval gut and mouth, are resorbed and eventually lost. The newly formed juvenile sinks to the sea floor and searches for a suitable crevice in which to hide. The young urchin stays there for four years until it reaches a diameter of about 4cm (1½in), when it is able to leave its crevice and survive the rigours of the open reef.

The common sea urchin does most of its growing over the summer months after it has spawned. During the winter it uses all its energy to build up the sex cells, with little left for growth. Like the trunk of a tree, the sea urchin's skeleton lays down annual rings, which can be counted to give a fair estimate of its age. An expert can 'read' these rings to give a record of the climatic conditions in the sea over the animal's lifetime.

A curious feature of sea urchin behaviour is that if one is disturbed – for instance, by being pulled off the reef and then replaced in the sea – it almost invariably starts to move upwards. The significance of the upward migration is almost certainly to enable the fallen animal to regain its place among its

COVERING UP

Some sea urchins exhibit a curious behaviour, which is known as 'hatting'. This is where an urchin uses its tube feet to pick up some shell, seaweed or other debris, which it then wears like a hat. There are numerous explanations for why they do this. The Greek philosopher Aristotle suggested that the extra weight acted as ballast to help hold the urchin down in rough seas. This is not very likely, as the tube feet are easily capable of anchoring the urchin to the rock.

Another possibility is that the covering acts as both camouflage and armour, protecting the urchin from predators that hunt by sight, and from those that feel for their prey. This would be particularly useful for the burrow-bound rock urchin. A further suggestion – that the urchins are using shell fragments and algae as sun-shades – is also a possibility. There are reports of urchins 'covering up' when exposed to strong light, and then taking off their 'hats' when it gets dark.

▲ The shore urchin is often seen wearing a 'hat' of shell or weed. The tube feet move debris this way and that, occasionally discarding it and picking up something else.

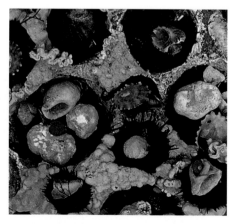

▲ Rock urchins grab all sorts of debris that comes their way. Edible morsels may be passed down to the mouth, but they hold on to larger objects, such as shells, perhaps as camouflage.

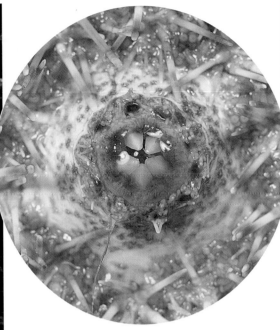

▲ Like other echinoderms, urchins have five long teeth, the tips of which just emerge from the mouth. These are part of the muscular feeding apparatus.

preferred food. This instinctive behaviour ensures that the sea urchin returns to shallow reefs if it has been washed away by a storm – or moved by divers.

Population pressures

The rock urchin, found mainly on the west coast of Ireland and on the French side of the English Channel, is widely regarded a culinary delicacy, superior to the edible urchin in terms of taste. Over the past 10 to 15 years both species have been consistently overfished so that now their numbers are seriously depleted.

As a result, much research into the farming of sea urchins has been undertaken. There have been advances in terms of developing suitable diets to

▲ A sea urchin's rate of growth depends on the amount of food available. Well-fed specimens have loosely plated shells to allow for future expansion, but the plates are fused in malnourished individuals.

ensure roe quality and colour, using pigments extracted from natural sources, such as microscopic algae. More recently, attention has switched to the shore urchin, which, despite its small size, has a potentially higher roe yield than either of the other two species. Urchin farming could soon be established, especially on the west coast of Scotland.

Another threat to sea urchins is the sale of tests and ornaments made from them, although trade has declined since the 1990s, perhaps because of an increased awareness of conservation issues.

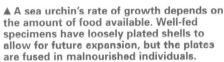

▼ At the top of the urchin, a cluster of small plates incorporate the anus, the genital pores and the 'madreporite', a sieve-like plate through which the urchin takes in water to its hydraulically operated system of tube feet.

▼ Urchin tube feet are amazingly elastic. They can reach out a considerable distance to sample the water chemically and by touch. In low oxygen conditions, the tube feet may be extended to allow respiratory gases to cross the very thin skin into the urchin's body.

Recognising coastal lichens

Along rugged western coasts that are bathed by humid, unpolluted sea breezes, colonies of lichens thrive on the upper shore, spreading imperceptibly year by year. They have been part of the maritime landscape for centuries.

U p until around 150 years ago, lichens were regarded as nothing more than simple, primitive plants. They were included in the same category as mosses and liverworts. However, when it was discovered that lichens were not a single organism but part fungus and part alga, they immediately acquired a separate status. To complicate matters, further research has shown that in this successful alliance, some lichen algae are, in fact, not algae at all but even more primitive organisms that belong to a major group of bacteria. Lichens are often referred to as symbionts, or 'partnership organisms'.

Beneficial combination
The visible body of a lichen – the thallus – comprises a compacted mat of hyphae, or fungal threads. The vast majority of lichens, as many as 98 per cent, belong to the group known as the Ascomycetes, in which spores are produced in special structures called asci. Cells of green algae or cyanobacteria are embedded within the thallus. There is usually just one species of alga or cyanobacterium per lichen.

Lichen fungi are not usually found living independently, whereas most partner species also occur as free-living entities. Both the fungal and the algal or cyanobacterial

Xanthoria parietina – better known by its common name, yellow scales – is one of the most widespread coastal lichens. It grows on rocks and walls and, despite its name, is often bright orange.

partner have a profound influence on the form the thallus takes, as well as on the exact habitat the lichen prefers and the range of chemical substances it produces. A lichen fungus provides its partner with a drier, brighter environment than it would find on its own and one that is relatively stable and safe. In return, the alga or cyanobacterium provides the organism with all the nutrients it needs.

Fungi are unable to manufacture their own food. Instead, they obtain nutrients from either decaying or living organisms, depending on the species. In the case of lichen fungi, they receive nutrients from their partners. Both green algae and cyanobacteria manufacture food by the chemical process known as photosynthesis, for which sunlight is essential. Consequently, almost all species grow in comparatively exposed locations, in order to receive as much sun as possible.

Slow growing
Lichens grow extremely slowly – they are perhaps the slowest growing of all living things. As a result, they are unable to colonise unstable locations, such as fast-eroding rocks. Most lichens also require high and fairly constant humidity. An abundance of solid, immobile and erosion-resistant rocks and boulders, together with the wet and windswept climate, makes the western coasts of the British Isles an ideal location. Coastal lichens can be found throughout much of the region.

EASY GUIDE TO SPOTTING COASTAL LICHENS

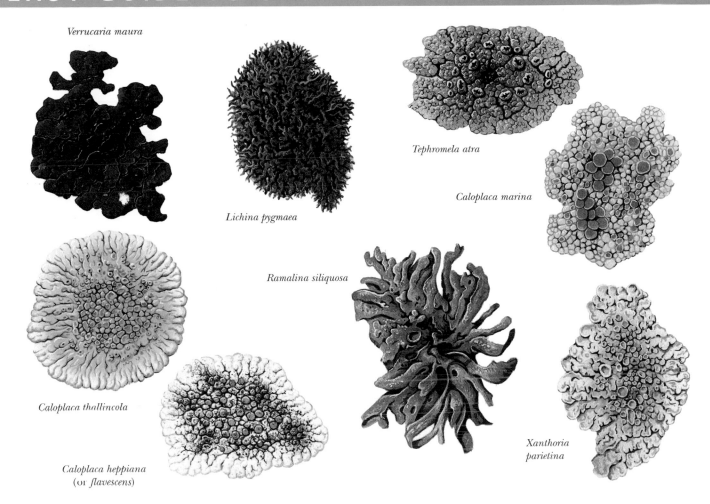

Verrucaria maura

Lichina pygmaea

Tephromela atra

Caloplaca marina

Ramalina siliquosa

Caloplaca thallincola

Caloplaca heppiana
(or *flavescens*)

Xanthoria parietina

WHAT ARE COASTAL LICHENS?

● A lichen is a small, long-lived organism comprising a fungus and an alga, or a primitive bacterium, living in a mutually beneficial partnership – this kind of relationship is known as symbiotic. The fungus, which does not look anything like other, separately growing, fungi, is dependent on its partner for survival.

● Reproduction is usually via spores produced by the fungus and dispersed by the wind or small animals, such as ants, slugs and beetles, to find a suitable algal or bacterial partner. In almost all species, the spores form in special cells (asci) that are contained within structures called apothecia, which grow on the main body of the lichen (the thallus).

● Some coastal lichens reproduce vegetatively, that is by a piece breaking off and starting to grow on a new surface, somewhere not too smooth and not too shaded. Many lichens are very brittle when dry and a fragment is easily dispersed by the wind or by birds looking for nesting material.

● Coastal lichens are able to colonise bare rock before other plants can do so. They start the process of breaking down rock, which leads to soil formation, and therefore have an important role to play in the ecosystem.

● The structure and shape of lichens conform to one of three basic types – fruticose, foliose or crustose. Fruticose lichens have a thallus that is tufted or bushy, and the upper and lower surfaces are identical in appearance. Foliose lichens have a leafy, rather flattened thallus and the upper and lower surfaces look different. In a crustose, or crustaceous, lichen, the whole thallus is attached to the surface on which it is growing.

● When lichens dry out they stop growing, starting again only when wetted.

● All lichens contain a number of chemicals, which are known collectively as 'lichen substances'. These generally give the lichens their colour.

HOW CAN I IDENTIFY COASTAL LICHENS?

● Lichens come in a wide range of colours and a seemingly endless variety of shapes. The type of thallus and the way in which the lichen is attached to the rock are clues to identity.

● Generally, crustose lichens predominate in areas that are subjected to the full force of the elements – wind, rain, snow and ice – and are important members of the lichen community on rocky coasts. Those growing near the sea look quite different from those growing inland on trees.

● A few specialised lichens, such as marine caloplaca, can tolerate immersion in sea water on a daily basis and another select group, including *Caloplaca thallincola*, can cope with being regularly dowsed with salt spray. However, many coastal lichens grow no lower down the shore than the splash zone, which is the area at the top of the upper shore, out of reach of all but the largest waves.

● A few species of coastal lichen have fruticose thalli, but these tend to grow farther up the shoreline, well out of reach of salty spray.

The centre of a lichen colony is generally the oldest part and frequently gets worn away while the edge is still growing.

Distribution map key

 Present all year round

 Not present

▶ Lichens are among the first organisms to colonise bare rock. They need very little water and are tolerant of extreme exposure to the elements.

▼ Man-made structures, such as sea defences, are just as suitable for lichen to grow on as natural rocks. Yellow scales is often one of the first to appear.

BLACK TAR   *Verrucaria maura*

Although black tar lichen often dominates rocky shores, it is easily missed because it looks just like tar. This crustose lichen grows around and below high-tide level, in a zone just above that occupied by barnacles. The surface of the thallus is dull black and crusty. Spores are produced in small flask-shaped structures, in this case called perithecia, sunk in the crust. The openings may just be visible as tiny raised dots, although these are even more difficult to see when the thallus is wet.

The aptly named black tar lichen often looks just like the results of a marine pollution incident. The edges of the thallus are irregular.

● SIZE
Extensive mats form a thin crust, often carpeting very large areas

● COLOUR
Black

● KEY FEATURES
Finely cracked surface texture

● HABITAT AND DISTRIBUTION
Usually grows between mid-tide and high-water marks; extremely common

BLACK TUFT   *Lichina pygmaea*

A fruticose lichen, black tuft is often abundant in the middle zone of a rocky shore, where patches of it grow in close proximity. The surface of the thallus, which has irregular edges, comprises densely packed, many-branched tufts. Although the lichen is mainly dark brown to black in colour, some of the branches are yellowish brown and flattened. Spherical apothecia, up to 2mm (⅛in) in diameter, form on the tips of the branches. When crushed, this lichen smells of embrocation.

Black tuft lichen resembles a miniature form of channelled wrack seaweed, but it usually grows lower down the shore.

● SIZE
Thallus tufts up to 1.5cm (⅝in) or more long

● COLOUR
Blackish brown

● KEY FEATURES
Densely tufted appearance

● HABITAT AND DISTRIBUTION
Grows in upper intertidal zone on rocky shores, often among barnacles; on exposed coasts, usually found on the middle zone of the shore

BLACK SHIELDS *Tephromela atra*

A pale to medium grey crustose lichen, black shields forms extensive patches on rocks and stone walls near the sea as well as inland. Colonies often abut each other and cover large areas. Each patch is surrounded by a faint bluish black line. The cracked, rough and often lumpy surface of the thallus is dotted with black-capped apothecia. The edges are irregularly lobed. This species is very similar to another, more exclusively coastal, lichen, *Lecanora gangaleoides*, but this can be distinguished by its more warty, darker greenish tinged thallus.

Raised, knobbly apothecia stud the surface of this lichen. These were known to 18th-century naturalists as 'shields'. Both parts of the scientific name also refer to the black appearance of these organs.

- **SIZE**
Thallus up to 15cm (6in) across, sometimes more
- **COLOUR**
Grey and black
- **KEY FEATURES**
Apothecia are raised black discs with thick grey rims. When cut open, they reveal a deep violet colour inside
- **HABITAT AND DISTRIBUTION**
Common on rocks and stone walls from splash zone upwards on rocky cliffs; also occurs inland

MARINE CALOPLACA *Caloplaca marina*

One of the most common and distinctive crustose seashore lichens, marine caloplaca is one of the few lichens that is tolerant of regular immersion in sea water. The surface of the thallus bears scattered granules, making it looked cracked and crusty, although the apothecia have smooth discs and rims. They are convex and deep reddish orange in colour. Another species, *Caloplaca maritima*, has a similar structure but is yellow or greenish yellow, never orange, and found in more sheltered spots higher up the shore.

In contrast to *Caloplaca heppiana*, marine caloplaca often forms scattered, irregular patches rather than neat rosettes.

- **SIZE**
Thallus up to 10cm (4in) across
- **COLOUR**
Yellowish orange or bright reddish orange
- **KEY FEATURES**
Granular surface and irregularly outlined thallus
- **HABITAT AND DISTRIBUTION**
Grows only on rocks and cement in walls in the splash zone from just above high-water mark; common

Caloplaca thallincola

A crustose lichen, *Caloplaca thallincola* forms distinctive rounded patches on hard rocks and is tolerant of occasional immersion by sea water. The thallus is often almost circular with a knobbly centre, and the edges of mature specimens are scored with radiating furrows. Convex apothecia up to a millimetre in diameter form in the centre of the thallus. They are orange with paler margins. This lichen prefers a more sheltered location than *Caloplaca marina*, but often grows on top of black tar lichen.

Like most other coastal lichens, *Caloplaca thallincola* can tolerate wind and rain. It can even cope with salt spray, but it cannot survive trampling feet. It is easily damaged or dislodged in popular tourist spots.

- **SIZE**
Thallus up to 10cm (4in) across
- **COLOUR**
Bright orange
- **KEY FEATURES**
Rounded thallus with deeply lobed margin
- **HABITAT AND DISTRIBUTION**
Favours rocks in splash zone and seldom found anywhere else; common

Caloplaca heppiana (or *flavescens*)

Caloplaca heppiana favours calcareous rocks, such as limestone, but it may occasionally be found growing on asbestos-cement and more rarely on brick. It is common on headstones in graveyards but is not often found on brick. The granular surface of the thallus is yellow and grey with orange spore-producing apothecia in the centre. When the centre falls out in mature specimens, it leaves a distinctly arc-shaped patch. This crustose lichen is found inland as well as near the coast. It is probably the commonest lobe-shaped species of *Caloplaca* in south-east England.

Caloplaca heppiana forms concentric patterns on rocks near the coast.

● SIZE
Thallus up to 6cm (2½in) across

● COLOUR
Variable, usually shows concentric zones of orange and yellow

● KEY FEATURES
In older specimens, central area of thallus sometimes starts to break down and wear away

● HABITAT AND DISTRIBUTION
On rocks, stone walls, concrete and wooden posts near the sea and inland; common

SEA IVORY *Ramalina siliquosa*

A distinctive fruticose lichen, sea ivory is branched and clump-forming. This is an extremely variable species. The clumps can be either tufty and erect or hanging in ragged-looking bunches. The branches of the thallus, which vary in colour from pale yellowish grey to darker greenish grey, are flattened and smooth. They are brittle to the touch, scimitar shaped and only a little divided above the base. The spore-producing apothecia are raised, often yellowish grey, discs.

Sea ivory forms matted tufts that grow so close to one another that they seem to form an almost continuous carpet. This provides valuable nutrients for grazing sheep in north Wales and Shetland.

● SIZE
Thallus up to 5cm (2in) long

● COLOUR
Greenish grey

● KEY FEATURES
Thallus branches are flattened and sometimes twisted; apothecia are terminal or sometimes lateral

● HABITAT AND DISTRIBUTION
On rocks near sea at high-water mark or above; common on coast, rare or absent inland

YELLOW SCALES *Xanthoria parietina*

A colourful and very distinctive crustose lichen, yellow scales dominates lichen communities on many British coasts. The thallus is knobbly and wrinkled in the centre but lobed at the edge. In mature specimens, the lobes are deeply and finely cut. Older yellow scales often overlap one another. This species is also widespread inland, where it grows on walls, trees and roofs, especially where the air is laden with dust containing mineral salts.

On exposed rocks and stones near the sea, yellow scales forms patches that are usually orange in colour, although they can vary from a darker orange to mid-yellow.

● SIZE
Thallus up to 15cm (6in) across

● COLOUR
Coastal forms are orange; inland forms are yellow, and paler than coastal ones

● KEY FEATURES
Forms rounded or broadly oval patches

● HABITAT AND DISTRIBUTION
Found from splash zone upwards on rocky cliffs, also on groynes, stone and brick walls and other man-made structures

Peaflowers

From late spring to early summer, clover-like peaflowers dot coastal paths, dry grassland and heaths. The flowers vary in colour from yellows to purples, sometimes even black.

Early season peaflowers are a distinct group of plants that come into bloom in late spring. Like the clovers, they belong to the pea and bean family, traditionally known as the Leguminosae, but now referred to as the Fabaceae. They have yellow, orange or red flowers, with the exception of lucerne, which has violet or reddish purple flowers.

Peaflowers are for the most part annuals, biennials and short-lived perennials, with a few longer-lived species. They are usually found on dry or well-drained soils, on grassland and on ground that has been previously cultivated.

Clues to identity

At first sight, members of this group may seem very similar. However, small but obvious characteristics of the leaves, flowers and especially the seed pods separate them. The leaves are mostly trifoliate – in threes – although the bird's-foot trefoils have an extra pair of leaflets at the base. In the bird's-foots and horseshoe vetch the leaves are pinnate – literally 'cut like a feather' – with small, narrow leaflets arranged along a common stalk. Kidney vetch has larger oval or elliptical leaflets, with a large terminal leaf.

The flowers are generally small, not more than 18mm (¾in) long. Each is typical of the pea family, with a five-toothed, tubular calyx of fused sepals and five unfused petals. The fruit is a pod, or legume, with one, two or many seeds.

Tricky medicks

The medicks, especially black medick, are easily confused with the small, yellow-flowered clovers, known as hop-trefoils. Medicks have a small tooth in

▲ **The yellow, orange or red flowers of kidney vetch often monopolise bare ground with suitable soil, such as chalk grassland, sand dunes and cliffs.**

the notch at each leaflet's tip. The flowerheads of the hop-trefoils turn brown as the fruit develops and the petals persist around each tiny, one-seed pod. Medick pods are not enclosed by petals and have two or several seeds.

Lucerne, the only medick with purple rather than yellow flowers, has escaped from cultivated land, where it is grown as alfalfa. On dry banks and roadsides in the Breckland of Norfolk, Suffolk and Cambridgeshire, the native sickle medick and introduced lucerne cross to form a bewildering array of intermediate hybrids. The flowers produced are of all colours, including yellows, greens, purples, bright greyish

▲ **Distinctive pods shaped like claws give bird's-foot its name. The dainty, inconspicuous flowers are usually self-pollinated.**

pink and even black – the only black flower in the wild flora of the British Isles.

Most peaflowers are widespread, although some of the medicks and bird's-foot trefoils are rare. Orange bird's-foot and slender bird's-foot trefoil are listed in the *Red Data Book* of Britain's rarest wild plants. Bird's-foot and hairy bird's-foot trefoil are in the *Irish Red Data Book*. Several other species are mainly southern or coastal in distribution.

PEAFLOWER FACT FILE

● Bird's-foot or least bird's-foot
Ornithopus perpusillus
Habitat and distribution
Widespread in dry grassland and on sandy heaths and waysides on lime-poor soils; in Ireland mostly in Co. Wexford and west Cork
Size 10–30cm (4–12in) long
Key features
Inconspicuous, usually prostrate, downy annual; leaves with 7–15 leaflets of equal size; flowers yellow, pink and white, 3–5mm (⅛–¼in) long, in stalked clusters of 3–8; pods 10–20mm (⅜–¾in) long, slender, slightly curved, constricted between seeds
Flowering time
May–August

● Orange bird's-foot
Ornithopus pinnatus
Habitat and distribution
Locally common on short turf on the Isles of Scilly
Size 10–40cm (4–16in) long
Key features
Similar to bird's-foot but leaves with far fewer leaflets; flowers orange-yellow, veined red, 6–8mm (¼–⅜in) long, in stalked clusters of 2–5; pods up to 3.5cm (1⅜in) long, slender, slightly curved, not constricted between each seed
Flowering time
March–September

● Common bird's-foot trefoil
Lotus corniculatus
Habitat and distribution
Dry grassland, sunny banks, rocky ground, sand dunes and lawns
Size 10–50cm (4–20in) tall
Key features
Prostrate, sprawling or erect, rather hairy perennial; leaves trifoliate with an extra pair of leaflets at base of stalk; flowers deep yellow, often tinged orange or red, 10–16mm (⅜–¾in) long, in stalked clusters of 2–7; pods 10–30mm (⅜–1¼in) long, cylindrical, arranged rather like bird's foot
Flowering time
May–September

● Narrow-leaved bird's-foot trefoil
Lotus glaber
Habitat and distribution
Scarce in short, dry grassland on lime-rich, often clay soils and by the sea, mostly in southern and south-eastern England
Size Up to 90cm (3ft) tall
Key features
Similar to bird's-foot-trefoil but taller and more slender, with narrow, less hairy leaflets; flowers 6–12mm (¼–½in) long, lemon yellow, mostly in heads of 2–4
Flowering time
June–August

● Greater bird's-foot trefoil or marsh bird's-foot trefoil
Lotus pedunculatus
Habitat and distribution
Marshes, ditches and damp grassland
Size Up to 100cm (40in) tall
Key features
Similar to bird's-foot-trefoil but hairier, taller and more erect with hollow stems; flowers in clusters of 5–12; calyx teeth of unopened flower buds spread out; pods up to 3.5cm (1⅜in) long
Flowering time
June–August

● Hairy bird's-foot trefoil
Lotus subbiflorus
Habitat and distribution
Dry, rocky grassland and coastal heaths in south-west England, south-west Wales, Co. Wexford and west Cork
Size Up to 30cm (12in) tall
Key features
Similar to bird's-foot-trefoil but a smaller, more slender, prostrate, very hairy annual; flowers orange-veined, 5–10mm (¼–⅜in) long, in clusters of 2–4
Flowering time
May–September

● Slender bird's-foot trefoil
Lotus angustissimus
Habitat and distribution
Dry, rocky or grassy places near the sea, in parts of southern and south-western England
Size Up to 80cm (32in) tall
Key features
Similar to hairy bird's-foot-trefoil but a slender, prostrate, downy annual; flowers a deeper yellow, 5–12mm (¼–½in) long, singly or in clusters of 2; pod 1–2cm (½–¾in) long
Flowering time
June–September

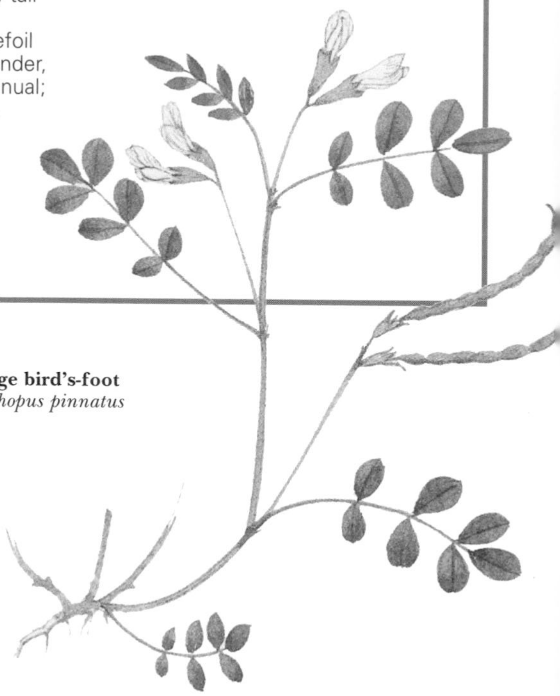

Orange bird's-foot
Ornithopus pinnatus

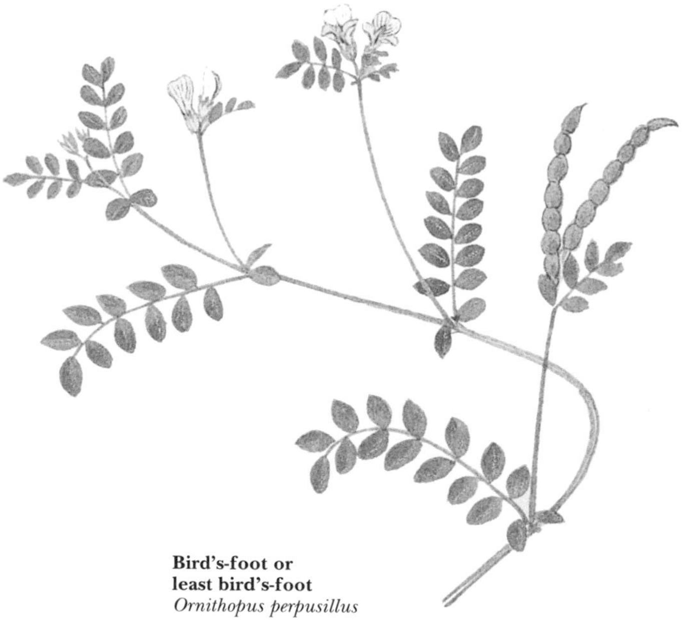

Bird's-foot or least bird's-foot
Ornithopus perpusillus

Bird's-foot trefoil has acquired many colourful local names such as eggs and bacon, butter and eggs, lady's fingers and granny's toenails. Some of these refer to the shape of individual flowers, others to the bright colours, while the long, claw-like seed pods have given rise to the rest.

Common bird's-foot trefoil
Lotus corniculatus

**Greater bird's-foot trefoil or
marsh bird's-foot trefoil**
Lotus pedunculatus

Narrow-leaved bird's-foot trefoil
Lotus glaber

Hairy bird's-foot trefoil
Lotus subbiflorus

Slender bird's-foot trefoil
Lotus angustissimus

PEAFLOWER FACT FILE

● Black medick
Medicago lupulina
Habitat and distribution
Common in dry, grassy and rocky places, on banks and sand dunes
Size 10–60cm (4–24in) long
Key features
Sprawling, downy annual, biennial or short-lived perennial; leaves trifoliate, oval, edges of leaflets serrated and end in tiny point; flowers yellow, 2–3mm (⅛in) long, unlike those of other medicks, held in stalked, almost spherical clusters; pods coiled and black when ripe, not covered by dead flowers
Flowering time
April–October

● Bur medick or small medick
Medicago minima
Habitat and distribution
Scarce and mainly coastal on open ground, dry banks and sand dunes in east and south-east England, from Norfolk to Kent
Size Up to 20cm (8in) long
Key features
Sprawling, densely downy annual or biennial; leaves trifoliate, oval, toothed near the tip; stipules (leaf-like organs at the base of the leaf stalk) untoothed; flowers yellow, 2–5mm (⅛–¼in) long, singly or in clusters of 2–6; pods often slightly downy, with spiral of 3–5 turns and double row of thin, hooked spines
Flowering time
May–July

● Spotted medick
Medicago arabica
Habitat and distribution
Dry, grassy or previously cultivated ground and sunny banks, mainly on sand and near the sea in south-east England, locally extending to northern Wales and south-east Scotland
Size 20–60cm (8–24in) long
Key features
Prostrate or sprawling, almost hairless annual; leaves trifoliate, heart-shaped, toothed, each with a conspicuous black blotch; flowers bright yellow, 4–6mm (⅛–¼in) long, singly or in clusters of 2–5; pods with spiral of 4–7 turns, hairless; very spiny
Flowering time
April–September

● Toothed medick or hairy medick
Medicago polymorpha
Habitat and distribution
Local on dry, open, sandy or gravelly places on coasts of East Anglia, south and south-west England and south-east Wales; also sometimes found inland on waste ground
Size Up to 30cm (12in) long
Key features
Similar to spotted medick but smaller and hairy; leaflets toothed only near the tip and with no black blotches; flowers 3–5mm (⅛–¼in) long, singly or in clusters of 2–8; pods on longer stalks, with spiral of 2–6 turns, and more deeply toothed stipules
Flowering time
May–September

● Sickle medick
Medicago sativa subsp. *falcata*
Habitat and distribution
Dry, open or grassy places and roadsides in Breckland and on coasts of East Anglia; introduced elsewhere
Size 20–60cm (8–24in) long
Key features
Sprawling or semi-erect, rather hairy perennial; leaves trifoliate, narrow, toothed; flowers yellow, 5–10mm (¼–⅜in) long, several in loose clusters; pods slightly or strongly curved; spineless, with 2–5 seeds
Flowering time
June–July

● Sickle medick and lucerne hybrids range in colour from yellow and green to violet and even black

● Lucerne or alfalfa
Medicago sativa subsp. *sativa*
Habitat and distribution
Relic of cultivation, naturalised on roadsides and cultivated or waste ground, except parts of north and west
Size 10–90cm (4–36in) tall
Key features
Similar to sickle medick but usually erect and flowers violet or reddish purple; pods coiled with spiral of 2–3 turns, 10–20 seeds
Flowering time
June–October

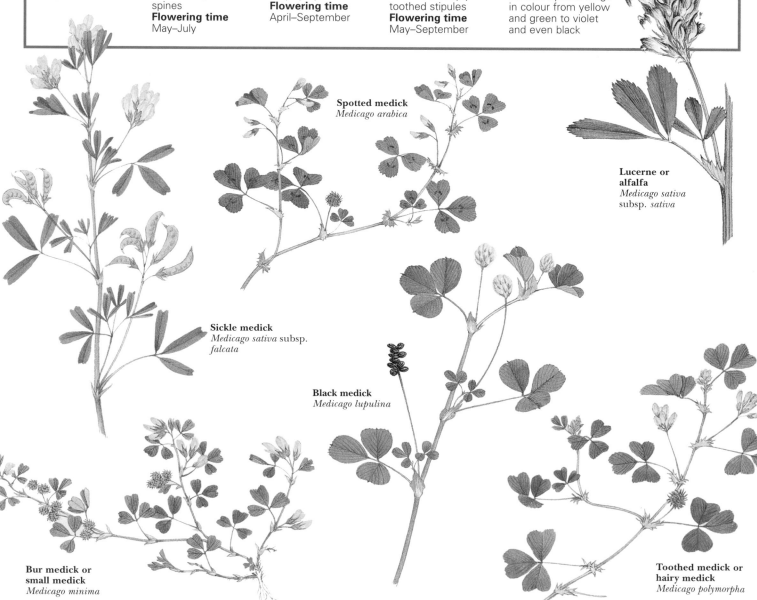

Spotted medick
Medicago arabica

Lucerne or alfalfa
Medicago sativa subsp. *sativa*

Sickle medick
Medicago sativa subsp. *falcata*

Black medick
Medicago lupulina

Bur medick or small medick
Medicago minima

Toothed medick or hairy medick
Medicago polymorpha

Horseshoe vetch grows mainly on calcareous soils, such as those of limestone cliffs and chalk downlands. It is a foodplant for the caterpillars of chalkhill blue and adonis blue butterflies.

PEAFLOWER FACT FILE

● Dragon's-teeth
Tetragonolobus maritimus
Habitat and distribution
A rare naturalised species introduced from central and southern Europe in dry grassland and on roadsides, mostly near the sea, from Gloucester to Essex and Kent
Size Up to 30cm (12in) tall
Key features
Like a robust bird's-foot-trefoil, but leaves more greyish green; flowers pale yellow, streaked brown and often reddish, solitary, 25–30mm (1–1¼in) long; pods 2–5cm (¾–2in) long, angled (like okra), winged
Flowering time
June–September

● Horseshoe vetch
Hippocrepis comosa
Habitat and distribution
Widespread on short grassland or rocky ground on chalk or limestone, mainly in southern England but north to Cumbria
Size 10–40cm (4–16in) tall
Key features
Sprawling or erect, hairy or nearly hairless perennial, slightly woody at base; 7–17 leaflets of equal size; flowers yellow, not tinged red, 5–10mm (¼–⅜in) long, in neat, stalked clusters of 5–12; pods 1.5–3.5cm (⅝–1⅜in) long, with horseshoe-shaped segments and tiny brown warts
Flowering time
May–July

● Kidney vetch
Anthyllis vulneraria
Habitat and distribution
Dry grassland, rocky ground, mountain ledges, sand dunes and roadsides, by the sea or on lime-rich soils
Size 10–60 cm (4–24in) tall
Key features
Sprawling to semi-erect, short-lived perennial; leaves with 3–9 oval or elliptical leaflets, silky, hairy beneath; flowers pale to deep yellow, also orange, cream, pink, reddish or purple, 12–15mm (½–⅝in) long, in dense heads, often in pairs, with ruff of leaf-like bracts below; pods egg-shaped, within persistent calyx
Flowering time
May–September

Dragon's teeth
Tetragonolobus maritimus

Kidney vetch
Anthyllis vulneraria

Horseshoe vetch
Hippocrepis comosa

WILDLIFE WATCH

Where can I find peaflowers?

● In spring, look in short grassland and on grassy heaths, on open or rocky ground and in grassy or slightly disturbed locations by the sea. Peaflowers mostly grow on lime-rich soils.

● Horseshoe vetch grows only on short chalk or limestone grassland, mostly in southern England. Greater bird's-foot trefoil grows in wet places and ditches, especially in the west and north. Orange bird's-foot is found on the Isles of Scilly.

Index

Photographs: Cover: otter: Brian Bevan/ardea.com, Wye Valley: David Woodfall/Woodfall Wild Images; Back cover: shelducks FLPA/T.Wharton; 1 Toad: NV/H.Angel; 2-3 Grey heron: John Daniels/ardea.com; 4 Osprey: FLPA/Fritz Polking; 5 Water meadow: PW, lobster: Sue Scott; 6(bl) NP/P.Craig-Cooper, (bc) NP, (br)NP; 7(blu) NP, (bl) NP, (br) NP/T.D.Bonsall; 8(bl) NP/R.Bush, (bc) NP/Paul Sterry, (br) NP/D.Smith; 9(bl) NP, (bc) NP, (br) NP/C.Carver; 10-11 Crowfoot David Woodfall/Woodfall Wild Images; 12(tr) ADT/B.Woods, (tc) OSF/S.Camazine, (b) Alamy/Edward Parker; 13(tl) NPL/K.Keatley, (tc) NPL/G.Dore, (tr) NPL/G.Dore, (bl) FLPA/J.Hawkins, (br) FLPA/N.Bowman, 14(tl) NV/H.Angel, (tc) PW/K.Preston-Mafham, (tr) Ecoscene/C.Gryniewicz, (cl) Ecoscene/R.Redfern, (bl) FLPA/D.A.Robinson, (bc) Ecoscene/A.Brown; 15(tl) NPL/M.Wilkes, (tc) PW/K.Prseton-Mafham, (tr) NP/P.Sterry, (b) PW; 16(b) Alamy/David Bartlett; 17(tr) Ardea/Chris Knights, (cr) BC/N.Blake, (c) Ardea/Robert T.Smith, (bl)Ardea, (br) BC/J.Jurka; 18(tc) Ardea/G.K.Brown, (tr) Ardea/I.Beames, (cl) BC/G.McCarthy, (c) Mike Read, (b) NP/Paul Sterry;19(tl) BC/U.Waltz, (bl) Ardea/D.Avon, (br) BC/F.De.Nooyer; 20(tc) BC/F.Labhart, (tr) Ardea/A.P Paterson, (cr) BC/R.Maier, (bl) BC/A.J.Purcell, (br) BC, (b) NP; 21(tl) BC/E.Pott, (br) BC/K.Taylor; 22(cl) NV/H.Angel, (bc) NV/H.Angel, (b) NHPA/D.P.Wilson; 23(tr) FLPA/D.P.Wilson, (cl) NV/H.Angel, (br) NHPA/John Bain; 24(l) NV/H.Angel, (tr)NHPA/R.Waller, (cl) Aquila, (c) NV/H.Angel, (b) WW; 25(bc) NV/H.Angel, (br) NV/H.Angel; 26(tl) NHPA/Trevor McDonald, (tr) FLPA/D.P.Wilson, (tc) NHPA/A.N.T, (cl) NHPA/Trevor McDonald, (cr) NHPA/E.A.Janes; 28(tr) NV/G.Kings, (bl) NP/C.Carver, (b) Alamy/Keith Pritchard; 29(tl) NP/P.Sterry, (tc)NP/C.Carver, (tr) OSF/B.Watts, (cr) Aquila/C.Smith; 30(tl) NP/R.Bush, (tr) Aquila/T.Leach, (cl) Windrush/D.Tipling, (b) NP/G.Du.Feu, (br) OSF/W.Gray; 31(tl) NP/P.Sterry, (tc) NV/K.G.Preston-Mafham, (tr)NP/E.A.Janes, (cr) NP/M.Lee, (bl) Laurie Campbell; 32(c) BC/C&S Hood, (b) Alamy/Chris Mole; 33(c) FLPA/S.Malowski, (tl) NP/P.Sterry, (br) NP/G.Du.Feu; 34(c) BC/D.Green, (b) WW/D.Woodfall; 35(tl) NP, (tc) NP, (tr) NP, (br) Ardea/Steve Hopkin; 36(tl) Mike Read, (tr) NP/P.Sterry, (b) WW/D.Woodfall, (br) NP/P.Sterry; 38-39 Sticklebacks: Ardea/Brian Bevan;40(l) Andy Rouse; 41(tr) BC/J.Burton, (b) WW/M&L Husar; 42(tr) OSF/R.Redfern, (bl) BC/R.Maier; 43(tr) Andy Rouse; 44(tl) NP/C.Carver, (tc) BC, (tr) BC, (bl) BC; 45(tl) FLPA/S.Malowski, (tr) NPL/L.M.Stone, (b) Andy Rouse;46(t) NPL/Tom Vezo; 47(r) FLPA/Michael Callen, (bl) BC/Heinrich van de Berg; 48(cl) NP/P.Sterry, (c) FLPA/Michael Jones, (cr) NP/Frank Blackburn, (bl) BC/Colin Varndell, (bc) Windrush/D.Tipling, (br) Windrush/Alan Petty; 49(cr) FLPA/W.Wisniewski; 50(t) FLPA; 51(tr) NP, (cr) NP, (cl) FLPA; 53(tl) NHPA/Stephen Dalton, (cl) FLPA, (bl) FLPA, 54(tl) NP, (cl) FLPA, (bl) NP; 55(c) FLPA/Fritz Polking; 56(bl) BC/Gordon Lansbury; 57(tr) Laurie Campbell, (cru) NHPA/Hellio & Van Ingen, (bl) Neil McKintyre; 58(tr) NP/Kevin Carlson, (br) BC/ Gordon Lansbury; 59(tc) OSF/Mike Brown, (tr) FLPA/Fritz Polking, (c) NP/W.S.Paton, (cr) BC/Mike Price, (br) Laurie Campbell; 60(bl) NP, (cr) Nick Giles; 61(tr) BC/H.Reinhard; 62(tr) Nick Giles, (cr) Nick Giles; 63(tr) Nick Giles; 64(r) NP/P.Sterry; 65(tr) Nick Giles, (c) Nick Giles, (cl) NP/Michael J. Hammett, (bl) Nick Giles; 66(t) Tom Walmsley; 67(cr) BC/Kim Taylor, (c) NP, (b) Tom Walmsley; 68(tr) BC/Kim Taylor, (cr) Tom Walmsley, (tc) BC/Kim Taylor, (cl) OSF/Richard Packwood, (bl) OSF/Mark Hamblin; 69(t) OSF/I.West, (bl) FLPA/H.D.Brandl; 70(cr) Laurie Campbell, (br) OSF/P.Franklin; 71(tl) NP/P.Sterry, (cl) NHPA/Stephen Dalton, (bl) NHPA/Stephen Dalton; 72(tl) OSF/F.Skibbe, (cr) NP/P.Sterry, (bl) NV/H.Angel; 73(tl) Windrush/C.Carver, (bl) Ardea/P.Steyn; 74(r) OSF/G.I.Bernard, (tr) OSF/Peter Gathercole; 75(tl) Nick Giles, (tr) Nick Giles, (cr) Nick Giles, (br) OSF/G.H.Thompson; 76(tr) NV/H.Angel, (b) NV/H.Angel; 77(br) NV/H.Angel; 78(cr) NV/H.Angel; 81 Puffin: John Cancalosi/ardea.com; 82(r) BC/George McCarthy; 83(c) BC/Peter Evans, (b) Mike Read; 84(b) BC, 85(r) BC; 86(l) NHPA/B.Coster; 87(c) FLPA/W.Wisniewski; 88(cl) NP/J.Karmali, (c) NP/R.Tidman, (cr) NP/M.Boulton, (bl) OSF/C.Knights, (bc) FLPA/R.Tidman, (br) NHPA/ J.L.Moigne; 89(tl) OSF/ E.Woods, (tr) BC/B.Glover; 90(tl) FLPA/E.Hosking, (tr) OSF/D.Tipling, (tl) OSF/M.Hamblin, (br) FLPA/T.Whittaker; 91(tl) BC/A.Potts, (b) FLPA/E.Hosking; 92(r) BC/Gordon Langsbury; 93(r) BC/Janos Jurka; 94(bl) FLPA/J.Watkins; 95(bl) FLPA/Ed Hosking, (tr) NP/P.Sterry; 96(tr) FLPA/R.Wilmhurst, (tc) NHPA/Andy Rouse, (tr) NP/P.Sterry, (cl) FLPA/Mike Jones, (c) David Boag, (cr) RSPB Photolibrary/Robert Horne, (bl) FLPA/D.Dugan; 97(tr) FLPA/P.Perry; 98(l) BC/T.Niemi; 99(tr) BC/G.Dore, (b)NP/R.Tidman; 100(tl) NP/P.Sterry, (tr) BC/D.Green; 101(tl) Aquila/J.Blossom, (tc) BC/D.Green, (cr) Aquila/H.Gebuis, (c) Windrush/J.Hollis, (cr) NHPA/A.Williams; 102(tr) FLPA/R.Wilmhurst, (bl) NP/ R.Tidman; 103(tr) BC/ B.Glover (b) FLPA/T.Wharton; 104(t) BC/Charles & Sandra Hood; 105(tr) OSF/ G.I.Bernard; 106(tl) OSF/ Fredrik Ehrenstrom, (cl) BC/ Eckart Pott, (br) BC/Frieder Sauer; 107(tr) OSF/Roger Jackman, (b) Sue Scott; 108(t) OSF/ P.Kay, (br) Sue Scott; 109(tr) NV/H.Angel, (cl) OSF/ J.A.L.Cooke, (cr) NV/H.Angel, (bl) FLPA/ D.P.Wilson; 110(t) NHPA/R.Waller; 111(tl) Sue Scott, (tr) Sue Scott, (bl) Sue Scott, (br) Sue Scott; 112(bl) Sue Scott, (br) Sue Scott; 113(tr) NV/H.Angel, (cr) FLPA/D.P.Wilson, (br) PEP; 114(cr) Sue Scott, (bl) Sue Scott, (bc) NV/ H.Angel; 115(tl) Sue Scott, (tr) NP/SC Bisserot, (bl) NV/H.Angel, (br) Sue Scott; 116(l) OSF/H.Taylor; 117(b) NV/ H.Angel; 118(tru) BC/P.Clement, (tr) NP/D.Osborn, (c) FLPA/ D.P.Wilson, (b) NV/H.Angel; 119 (t) NHPA/ G.I.Bernard, (c) NHPA/ L.Campbell, (b) Ecoscene/C.Gryniew, 120(t) NV/H.Angel, (c) WW/S.Austin, (b) FLPA/D.Hall; 121(t) NP/P.Sterry, (cr) NP/P.Sterry; 122(br) FLPA/E&D Hosking; 125(tl) Andrew Gagg.

Illustrations: 43(b) John Ridyard; 52(t) Tim Hayward; 53(tr) Tim Hayward, (cr) Tim Hayward, (br) Tim Hayward; 54(tr) Tim Hayward, (cr) Tim Hayward, (br) Tim Hayward; 94(tl) John Ridyard: 97(bl) John Ridyard; 100(b) John Ridyard; 117(t)The Art Agency/Myke Taylor; 122(c) Ian Garrard.

Key to Photo Library Abbreviations: BC = Bruce Coleman Ltd, FLPA = Frank Lane Photo Agency, GPL = Garden Picture Library, NHPA = Natural History Photo Agency, NI = Natural Image, NP = Nature Photographers, NPL = Nature Picture Library, NSc = Natural Science Photos, NV = Heather Angel/Natural Visions, OSF = Oxford Scientific Films, PW = Premaphotos Wildlife, WW = Woodfall Wild.

Key to position abbreviations: b = bottom, bl = bottom left, blu = bottom left upper, br = bottom right, bru =bottom right upper, c = centre, cl = centre left, clu = centre left upper, cr = centre right, cru = centre right upper, cu = centre upper, l = left, r = right, sp = spread, t = top, tl = top left, tlu = top left upper, tr = top right, tru = top right upper.

Wildlife Watch
Waterside & Coast in Spring

Published by the Reader's Digest Association Limited, 2005

The Reader's Digest Association Limited
11 Westferry Circus, Canary Wharf
London E14 4HE

We are committed to both the quality of our products and the service we provide to our customers, so please feel free to contact us on 08705 113366, or via our website at: www.readersdigest.co.uk

If you have any comments about the content of our books you can contact us at: gbeditorial@readersdigest.co.uk

Reader's Digest General Books:
Editorial Director Julian Browne
Art Director Nick Clark
Series Editor Christine Noble
Project Editor Lisa Thomas
Project Art Editor Julie Bennett
Prepress Accounts Manager Penelope Grose

This book was designed, edited and produced by Eaglemoss Publications Ltd, based on material first published as the partwork *Wildlife of Britain*

For Eaglemoss:
Project Editor Marion Paull
Editors Paul Brewer, Celia Coyne, Samantha Gray, John Woodward
Art Editor Phil Gibbs
Editorial Assistant Helen Hawksfield
Consultant Jonathan Elphick

Publishing Manager Nina Hathway

Printed and bound in Europe by Arvato Iberia

CONCEPT CODE: UK 0133/G/S
BOOK CODE: 630-010-01
ISBN: 0 276 44058 7
ORACLE CODE: 356200014H.00.24